PARADOX L

Unearthing God in an Age in
Which We Are Enslaved
to Dogma and Drowning in Relativism

Thomas V. Lyons

© 2024 by
Thomas V. Lyons

Unless otherwise marked Scripture quotations are taken from the Amplified Bible (amp), Copyright © 2015 by The Lockman Foundation. Used by permission. lockman.org

Scripture quotations marked (csb) have been taken from the Christian Standard Bible, Copyright © 2017 by Holman Bible Publishers. Used by permission. Christian Standard Bible and CSB are federally registered trademarks of Holman Bible Publishers.

Scripture quotations marked (niv) are taken from the Holy Bible, New International Version, NIV. Copyright © 1973, 1978, 1984, 2011 by Biblica, Inc.™ Used by permission of Zondervan. All rights reserved worldwide. www.zondervan.com

Scripture quotations marked (ampc) taken from the Amplified Bible (ampc), Copyright © 1954, 1958, 1962, 1964, 1965, 1987 by The Lockman Foundation Used by permission lockman.org

All emphasis in Scripture has been added by the author.

Cover and diagram design by Bryan Butler Studio

Table of Contents

Introduction 1
THE JOURNEY: A LONG SHOT | Curiosity killed the cat 6
1 | At Home 7
2 | In Undergrad 9
3 | A Janitor 12
4 | Biblical Theology and the Trinity 20
5 | My Political Awakening 24
6 | Truth: Round One 27
7 | The Arrival 33
THE HOLY SPIRIT: A SNAPSHOT | What came first, the chicken or the egg? 39
8 | An Introduction 40
9 | Genesis 1:2 45
10 | Freedom and Energy 48
11 | Experiment and Explore 52
12 | Reproduction and Multiplication 55
13 | Comfort and Restore 58
14 | Art and Dreams 60
15 | Liberalism 68
16 | Emotions 70
17 | Female 72
18 | Conclusion 75
THE FATHER: A SLAP SHOT | The Tortoise and the Hare ... 80
19 | An Introduction 81
20 | Father 90
21 | Ideal and Judge 92
22 | Strive and Produce 95
23 | Function and Understanding 100
24 | Structure and Protection 102
25 | The Brain 106
26 | Competition 108

27 | Leadership 113
28 | Personality 115
29 | Conclusion 117
30 | The Father and the Holy Spirit 119
THE FOOL: A MUG SHOT | Why did the chicken cross the road? 128
31 | An Introduction 129
32 | Speaking Truth to Pain 130
33 | Speaking Truth to Power 134
34 | The Fool to Master: Part One 136
35 | The Joker 140
THE SON: A FLU SHOT | Give a man a fish, feed him for a day. | Teach a man to fish, feed him for a | lifetime.—Old adage 144
36 | An Introduction 146
37 | The Seed and Embodiment 151
38 | The Willful Sufferer 158
39 | The Mediator 170
40 | The Truth: Round Two 174
41 | The King 178
42 | The Fool to Master: Part Two 184
43 | The Judge Redeemer 189
44 | The Door 195
45 | Communication 200
46 | Psychology 208
47 | Education 210
THE SHADOW: A POT SHOT | Don't put all your eggs in one basket. 215
48 | An Introduction 216
49 | Arrogance and Tyranny 220
50 | Resentment and Anarchy 223
51 | Sexuality 233
52 | Love 240
Conclusion 246

To Mom and Dad, who first introduced me to the God of the Bible.

Introduction

I was in a new town, in a new building, with new people. I was about six years old.

Because I was sitting with my family, I was comfortable, up until the moment that the children my age were expected to leave that room and go to another part of the building. When I looked over at my family for support, they all waved me to the door.

By the time I left, there were no other children present that I could follow out of the room. As I walked away from my family and made my way toward the door, fear began to grip me. I saw the door, but I didn't know where it led. I had no idea how to navigate through the new space to get wherever it was I was supposed to be.

I stepped through the large door and passed to the other side. The door closed behind me. The light was dim. Tears began to wet my cheeks. I was alone, in a new town, in a new building, in a new space in the building, with no further direction.

The difference between the Philosophers mind and everyone else's, is everyone else has nature and history as their basis for normalcy. So, when something anomalous or out of the ordinary occurs that demands attention and explanation, it's in relation to or in contrast with the norms in nature and/or history.

The philosophers mind, on the other hand, has nothingness as his or her basis for normalcy. So, that there is anything and that anything has particularity is the anomaly. Which means anything and/or everything deserves investigation and explanation. Why is there anything and why is it what it is?

"Why is there something rather than nothing?", truly is the lens through which the philosopher sees.

The Theologians presupposition is that God created with great intention and meaning.

The philosopher coupled with the theologian, then, should lead us to this moment in our society when we are asking fundamental questions related to the nature of the human, the differences in sexuality, morality in politics and so on.

What should be highest? What should be named God, the king among kings? self-expression, tolerance and compassion? Or facts, law and order?

So, where are the philosophers, and why do the theologians insist on parroting irrelevant religious mantras in the face of our society's deterioration?

We're lost without the philosophers and stuck without a deeper relevant theology.

When your math teacher asks you to show your work, what are they asking?

If the math student has the right answer but cannot demonstrate how they arrived there, then they do not know what they ought.

Having the right answer is hardly the aim. It's not quite beneficial.

If the expectation of showing your work is removed, then having the right answer slowly becomes relative.

Christianity is in a moment that is preceded by a few centuries in which no one has requested of it to show its work. As a result, we Christians now have no idea how to get to the right answer that we claim to have.

No wonder relativism has taken root.

Friedrich Nietzsche, 19th century philosopher and critic of Christianity was right, "God is dead."

He believed that modern man disposed of the need for the religious domain. He argued that as a result, it would usher in an oscillation between totalitarianism and nihilism, hierarchy and equality. It would produce horrors only found in descriptions of hell.

Here we sit on the other side of the 20th century, the bloodiest in recorded history.

Here Christianity sits, in a culture that doesn't know what a woman is and has no compelling reason for its claims of absolutes. The West is now drowning in relativism, dogma, ideology, and tribalism . . . and that's just our theologians!

There is a true sense in which for the last few centuries our society has been running on the fumes of the Christian worldview that helped build it. It seems quite evident now that those fumes have dissipated.

I would argue that Christianity in the west today, is running on the fumes of its doctrinal depths and advances of the past. It is marked by dogma and tradition, psychobabble and wishing.

The fundamental questions and answers that have been assumed for so long about the world and our existence, being asked in our growing secular culture, have been responded to by Christianity with religious cliché's.

The responses have little to no connection to the world and its varying fields of study. Perhaps this is because modern western Christianity itself has followed right behind in the severance of the sacred and secular.

There has been a growing distance between modern Christianity and the depths of and roots in the knowledge of God.

> In our modern forms of specialized education there is a tendency to lose the whole in the parts, and in this sense, we can say that our generation produces few truly educated people. True education means thinking by associating across the various disciplines, and not just being highly qualified in one field, as a technician might be. I suppose no discipline has tended to think more in fragmented fashion than the orthodox or evangelical theology of today.
>
> —Francis Schaeffer, *The God Who Is There* (Chicago, Illinois: InterVarsity Press, 1968), 32.

That is a devastating critique.

I grew up as an evangelical pastor's kid. I knew all the Sunday School answers. Yet Christianity hadn't helped me sort out my own significant shortcomings. Where exactly was salvation?

Christianity has grown and flourished but is now withered and decayed. It's irrelevant. Which means, God is irrelevant. That is an oxymoron. We must be missing something; something about God and something about us.

Passion, dogma, or sincerity does little to highlight truth in a relativistic age.

Having the right answer, while pointing our finger at secularism and post-modernism ends up being self-incriminating.

If we don't take issue with ourselves first, as the blind absolutists, or spineless universalists, then any outcries against evil will just expose our ignorance and self-righteousness.

We can blame the truth holders that we inherited the cliches from, but they are dead and gone. We are here now. Are we going to do the work necessary to unearth the reasons why the truth we claim to have is good and eternal?

God is the eternal good. He is the creator of all things. All created reality is good because it is about Him, patterned after Him, and hence, for Him.

The cosmic design and function come from the realities that define God and His function.

All truth is God's truth. There is no truth present at any point, at any level of analysis, in any field of study, that doesn't find its roots, its origin in the nature and character of the triune God. If you understand who God is, you will understand why whatever the truth is, is true. If you want to understand God, figure out why the truth anywhere is true.

> Common grace assures us that no worldview is entirely mistaken; the pervasive power of sin assures us that no worldview in any way removed from Scripture is benign. Let God be true, and every worldview a

liar.—D. A. Carson "The Dangers and Delights of Postmodernism", *Modern Reformation*, July/August 2003. https://www.modernreformation.org/resources/articles/the-dangers-and-delights-of-postmodernism

This is my journey, deep below the surface. Come along. Join me as I retrace some of my steps to what I discovered.

THE JOURNEY: A LONG SHOT
Curiosity killed the cat.

1
At Home

It's 2018, northwest side of inner-city Chicago. I'm at a local diner, sitting across from a lifelong friend who leans in across the table from me. With concern, he asks, "Are you stuck?"

In the span of just a few months, a handful of those closest to me, expressed in similar language the possibility that I may be in a bad place. A place that if I didn't move away from or get out of, could lead to some chaotic, disturbing, dark unknown.

"Are you stuck?"

I heard them, but I was somehow getting in my own way.

I'm an introvert. I'm an inward, slow processor. This means, there are thoughts that I will consider for a long time before speaking or taking action.

Most of the time I have no idea what to say or how to respond because I haven't sorted out the words in my head yet. For an inward processor, it is already determined that no words come out before some words get organized, checked, and then "okayed" before being released.

I have an affinity for the past.

I'm conservative; not a risk taker.

I'm orderly. I like things to be organized. I need structure. I thrive in systems.

I'm competitive. Competition motivates me.

I'm task oriented.

You get the generic picture.

It's been several years since graduating from college. I haven't pursued a position in my field, church ministry. The jobs I've worked have been in manual labor. Give me a broom or a box to move and I'll be more than content.

It was never clear to me whether I was avoiding something, perhaps out of fear.

I was born into a Christian family. My dad was pastor of a Baptist Church on Chicago's northwest side. Being in the heart of Chicago and in a church that reflected the diverse neighborhoods that mark the north side certainly helped round out my experience and vision of the world.

However, a significant aspect of my identity could be marked by the evangelical Christianity of our generation. I'm as comfortable in and around church and Christian life as anyone. Being a pastor's kid definitely adds a layer of exposure.

For better or worse, I am a product of our twenty-first-century Christianity.

When I decided as a junior in high school to pursue a vocation in Christian ministry, it was a stamp on the appreciation I had for my heritage. So, the path forward seemed clear enough.

Yet, here I was, years later, seemingly a victim of my own anxieties.

There seemed to be conflict within, slowing me down and hindering me from moving forward toward my goal.

Part of it was I was busy analyzing my own life, along with the Christian worldview it was set in.

"Are my reservations good?"

"Are my conservative tendencies righteous?"

"Does my orderliness and high view of authority match the Christian explanation?"

"Will my approach to life produce the good things I desire out of life?"

"Are the best Christian and theological explanations today the best to be had?"

My drive to question and contemplate led me on this journey. I had no idea it would lead me where it did.

2
In Undergrad

After high school, I landed in Louisville, Kentucky, on the campus of the Southern Baptist Theological Seminary. Boyce College was the undergrad school.

There are a few notable elements that had a significant impact on me and this journey while attending there.

For starters, there were a couple of classes—Worldviews and a course in Theology and Culture—that really resonated with me.

Up until those two classes I always wondered about my proclivity to think. Each professor in both classes emphasized the element of being able to process and develop as a critical thinker. This helped affirm, to some degree, that not only was I not weird, but I had a tendency toward a value that could be used for good.

Another course, Theology III, I took with Dr. Russell Moore, who was the vice president of the seminary at the time. I'll never forget the opening lecture. It changed my understanding forever.

Dr. Moore drew a horizontal line across the whiteboard. He put a cross somewhere in the middle of the line and went on to explain how all things, all of history is taken into account by the narrative found in the Scripture. The central message, called the gospel or good news, of the Scripture narrative, is the central element to all things.

In order for me to understand something at all, I typically have to understand the whole as well as its individual parts at the same time.

I grew up in church. I knew the Bible stories. I had spent endless hours at that point digging into Christian teaching and lifestyle. But how did it all come together and resonate with all reality?

Dr. Moore initiated for me the idea that this central message found in the Christian Bible was the central reality from which all things find their ultimate meaning.

I spent the next several years thinking about and building into this idea.

Dr. Moore operated from this underlying framework when lecturing and preaching. One of his sermons that played a significant role in my pursuit of understanding this framework was on Christ and marriage from Ephesians chapter 5.

There were a couple of key concepts that I took from his sermon.

First, marriage was patterned after what God was doing in history, namely, Christ's death, burial, and resurrection. Dr. Moore explains that Paul's comparison between marriage and Christ and His church is not arbitrary.

He argues that marriage itself is being produced by the underlying framework of what Christ is and is doing with His church. When God institutes marriage at the beginning of the Scripture narrative, He's using the Christ crucified, resurrected, and coming again framework, even though Christ has not entered into the history storyline to accomplish that yet.

Second, Dr. Moore emphasizes the priority of union in marriage and the gospel, and that it plays a central role in how the gospel functions.

The point of marriage is union. Two becoming one.

That element is coming from the reality of Christ being united to His church. And we see that language emphasized through the book of Ephesians and the rest of Paul's letters in the Bible.

Union wasn't just an add on but played a central role in what God was doing in history and how the institution of marriage was designed to operate.

As I continued to process, there was a word, a question that became a useful tool in my journey down into the depths of theology and reality.

The question was "Why?"

"Why?" gets you behind and underneath any who, what, where, or how. It leads you as far behind or underneath as you would like to go.

So, critical thinking, the gospel as central, the concept of union, and the question "why?" were tools and ideas that I took with me after I graduated and moved back to Chicago. They would play a vital role for the next several years as I searched deeper for truth.

3
A Janitor

Back in Chicago, I was job hunting for a few months. After several offers and job interviews, I landed at my home church working under the facilities superintendent.

The job included everything from cleaning, maintenance, and construction. This allowed me the next several years to spend endless hours listening to sermons, debates, lectures, podcasts, and so on. One year I listened through the entire Bible four times.

As I listened through varying material hour after hour, I was thinking and processing. It wasn't just background noise. I was fully engaged in whatever it was I was listening to.

One of the areas I quickly grew interested in and spent several years diving into was the debate of God's existence. It was fascinating, not only because it was a discussion that has been going on for millennia, but because we live in a time and culture where religion and theology are criticized for not being serious disciplines.

We live in an age of skepticism. Science and modern technology are what we believe in. Religion and theology are for ancient people who knew nothing about the world like we know now. The religious domain is put on the same level as belief in Santa Claus or the Easter Bunny.

Attending atheist debates seemed like a natural path to take if I wanted to grow in my ability to think critically about what I held as most important, namely God and His message.

I'll never forget the first debate I came across on YouTube on the subject. It was between William Lane Craig and Frank Zindler.

I was taken aback by how weak the argument for atheism was in light of William Lane Craig's case for God and Christianity. The strengths and weaknesses of the arguments didn't seem to mirror the popular culture and higher education's consensus on the matter.

I am biased of course. Who isn't? But as I listened to several hours' worth of debates on the subject over the next several years, I grew in critical thought. When I heard a weak argument from the side I favored, I would note it. When I heard substantive argumentation from the opposing side, I would note it.

I was not interested in simply receiving a pat on the back by content that affirmed what I already thought. I was interested in figuring out what the truth was.

I realized that the sign that someone truly valued the truth, would not be found simply in their ability to defend what they knew and believed, but their willingness to critique it. If what they had was true, then it would be able to withstand the harshest judgment.

Critical thinking drove my curiosity and pursuit of truth. I used the question "why?" like a shovel that calloused my hands.

As I moved from floor to floor, room to room, cleaning in that old church building, I spent hours and hours listening through Christian sermons, oftentimes listening through the same sermon or sermon series several times.

I tuned into preachers who tended to explain the central message of the Scripture. Preachers like John Piper, Russell Moore, John MacArthur, Ryan Fullerton, to name a few.

I wasn't as interested in the practicality of the content and how it applied immediately to me, although I took all I could get. I was interested in understanding why the gospel message would resonate at all.

What was the nature of this particular explanation, the gospel, the so-called ultimate truth?

I continued to grow in understanding. Not only that the Christian message was accurate but could only be true if it was the central and fundamental explanation of literally everything.

The more I listened and analyzed, the more I was convinced that this central message of Christianity was a far more superior explanation than any other I had encountered. At the same time, the more I learned and understood, new questions would arise. So, the need to continue to go deeper and journey further remained.

What was the central message of the Bible, and could it be summed up?

The Christian message, the gospel, can be summed up in five points. I took this from my church youth pastor.

1. God: He is the greatest entity; eternal, all good, creator of all things.

2. Man: made in the image of God; made to reflect God and be in perfect relationship with Him.

3. Sin and Penalty: Man rebelled against God, resulting in death, eternal separation from God.

4. Jesus: God in flesh, came to earth to die, be buried and rise, on behalf of the sinner.

5. Repentance and Faith: Man's response for salvation, be reunited to God by; acknowledgment of guilt of sin and putting trust in Jesus for new life.

What seemed to make the most sense was the idea that in order for the gospel to be true, in all the ways it claimed and at varying levels of analysis, it had to be the foundation upon which all of created reality was built. It had to be the root from which all of natural reality has been produced.

So, when God is creating, He is patterning the created order and history after the points, the elements that make up the Christian message. This is an incredible concept.

Paul's point when he makes his case for marriage in Ephesians, is that when God creates at the beginning and institutes marriage, He is using the blueprint of Christ and His church to do it.

That doesn't seem natural at first glance because It's obvious that Christ and the Church come on the scene so far later in the storyline. It seems like God is getting the idea for Christ and the church from marriage. But when you have a writer/director, who is orchestrating all things, He can unfold the story in that manner.

As I listened through those sermons, this was the argument I was hearing them make.

The gospel message was the foundation or the central theme for the existence and meaning of all things. I began to jot down different ways of stating this idea. Here are a few.

The gospel is central to all of life.

The gospel makes sense of everything.

The gospel is the interpretive key to understanding the mysteries of the universe, all areas of life, and human experience.

God designed, with the elements and realities of the gospel woven into the fabric of the created order and human experience; so that the meaningfulness of life is found as it relates to, is connected to, based on, reflective or a copy of, the realities of the gospel.

The gospel is not only the rescue plan for sinners, or the prescription for saints, but is also the DNA of the created order, human existence, and experience.

The gospel is the DNA of creation, the rescue plan for sinners, and the prescription for saints.

The gospel is central to all things in two ways:

First, all of history is God's doing and under His orchestration, in which Christ's death, burial, and resurrection is the theme. This means everything in the universe, including the individual, plays a role in God's grand story of history.

Second, the elements, both great and significant, small and insignificant, that make up life experiences, individually reflect and point to the great narrative story of Christ and the church.

Here are a couple of examples of the Christian message being the root of reality.

A preacher once explained the purpose of marriage with five P's: Purity, Partnership, Procreation, Pleasure, Picture.

With the framework that marriage was patterned after the gospel, I began to process these five P's and see if they aligned with what I understood the gospel to entail. They appeared to line up very well.

If you pushed each of those terms to their end you would land where the gospel says its message is leading. Namely, a place or condition that is

Pure—right clean.

Partnership—in relationship.

Procreation—ongoing life, future, hope.

Pleasure—happiness.

Picture—something larger than itself, tied to an eternal highest.

I jotted down synonyms of each of those "P" words. Then I decided to jot down antonyms of each of those words. What I discovered was that the description when you put all of those antonyms together was something like hell: polluted, alone, dead end, pain, and meaninglessness.

That's an example of how the makeup of the reality we all acknowledge as real and meaningful, to whatever degree, is connected to and rooted in this Christian explanation we call the gospel.

One more example.

The gospel being central to all of reality and desire to see and show its consistency, was a thought I developed after hours of listening to atheists debates.

From my biased position, it seemed as though no matter how well the opposing argument was constructed, the proponent for atheism was fixed in his position. Yet their most often and strong response was that there was not sufficient evidence for the existence of God.

So, I came up with this question for the atheist or agnostic: "What would you require as sufficient evidence for the existence of God?"

Now, this question seeks to take into account the atheist's worldview, oftentimes being naturalistic.

After listening to varying kinds of ideas for evidence proposed by atheists of God's existence that they would be more likely to believe, I realized how insufficient they were. Things like, "If God came down right now," or, "If God wrote in the sky with the stars, 'I am real.'"

Evidence such as these would be fairly easy to ignore or explain away.

I began to think about what I would require if I were trying to hold to a naturalistic worldview and wanted to figure out what would be the strongest evidence for God. I came up with the concept of incarnation and resurrection. Not Jesus' incarnation or resurrection, but the concepts.

Anything short of God becoming a human and stepping into history, where He could be related to, talked with, watched, observed, could be disregarded as not enough.

Becoming a historical figure is important because it places Him at the same level of scrutiny as any other verifiable reality that we judge things by. If He showed up out of thin air for a moment or wrote a message in the sky, that would be far less substantive than becoming a historical figure.

He would then have to do something that we would acknowledge as the most difficult according to anyone's standards. Being dead and then coming back to life after a few days, would be in that category. Now, death isn't just physical, it resonates with the human on the emotional, psychological, spiritual, levels. It's the greatest enemy of humans.

In short, the Christian documentation and explanation has in it a degree of evidence for the existence of God that is sufficient according to anyone's standards, including the historians, the humanists, the psychologists, the naturalists, the religious, the scientist, and so on.

For the moment, whether you believe the offered content as actual or not doesn't matter. Conceptually, you can't come up with a higher degree of evidence to be required. You could add to it, but you can't up the degree of it.

I state it this way: if you locked twelve naturalistic atheists in a room and they did not come out until they provided the best evidence they would require for the existence of God, through all of their propositions, discussions, critiquing, and brainstorming, the concepts of incarnation and resurrection would be on their final list.

Journeying down and arriving at this level of understanding and explanation about the Christian worldview was extremely satisfying.

If the true worldview was analyzed, it would have to resonate at all levels of analysis. It would have to be the source and foundation for all that is. It would have to bring an explanatory power to every field of study no matter how small or great in detail.

To spend several years analyzing and critiquing Christianity and begin to see how all things were tying together, was extremely meaningful.

What God was doing with Jesus and His salvation plan was the blueprint for all of reality. What a framework!

After years of thinking through that concept, at some point along the way, I realized that blueprint wasn't the bottom level.

A question arose in my mind—Jesus and His salvation plan are something particular. Why this plan? Where was it coming from?

I know it was coming from God. It was His plan, and He is the one who instituted it. But why the particulars of this plan, centered around Jesus, and operating in this way?

Why create?

Why male and female or any particular that makes up a human?

Why the long length of time between the garden and the Messiah?

Why sacrifice and suffering?

My initial thought was that God didn't do anything arbitrarily and certainly not the most important things. Everything He did was initiated and birthed out of who and what He was.

But what was it about God that produced what we understand the gospel to be; what the created order, history and the human experience is?

What was the gospel message standing on? Where was it coming from? Why was it something particular and what gave those particulars meaning?

So, although I followed the theologians down to this point, that the central message of the Scripture is the foundation and meaning for all things, I realized that I could inquire further.

4
Biblical Theology and the Trinity

There were two elements that played important roles as I continued drilling down beneath the central message of the Scripture narrative.

The first was developing an understanding of the entirety of the Scripture story.

In my second year of college, I read through the Bible in a year for the first time. The point was not to spend time going in depth but rather to read at a quick pace to get the overall picture. That was one of the most beneficial studies I've done.

It's a lot of content. To see it all in one shot, as well as the parts, characters, and individual stories that make it up, really brings tremendous understanding.

When you put a jigsaw puzzle together, one of the first things you do is look at the picture depicted on the box that shows what the completed puzzle looks like. As you put the pieces together you reference the completed picture to help guide and test whether or not you are putting the pieces together correctly.

In his podcast lecture series on his Systematic Theology book, Wayne Grudem has seven lectures on how to interpret the Bible. In those lectures, he discusses what Biblical theology is.

Biblical theology is viewing the Bible as a single unit, and how all of the different parts, books, characters, stories, and themes are coming together and operating in unison to make up one large narrative. The entire scriptural narrative is centered around the person and work of Jesus.

This view of the Bible, as an unfolding story in which all of its parts are linked and supporting one another, really helped me get a handle on the Bible.

Around the same time, I read a book titled *Preaching Christ from the Old Testament* by Sidney Greidanus. He walks through a hermeneutical structure which explains how the Old Testament is about and moving toward Jesus. Jesus isn't just hinted at or mentioned a few times throughout the Old Testament. The Old Testament is playing the crucial role of laying the foundation and being uniquely positioned to produce Jesus as the Messiah. In theological circles we call it seeing, teaching, or preaching Christ from all of Scripture.

The Village, written and directed by M. Night Shyamalan, is one of my favorite movies.

It involves a group of people who live in a small village. As the movie unfolds, you grow accustomed to their living arrangements, clothing style, speech patterns, and way of life. You quickly learn of the threat lurking in the woods that surround the village and the precautions they take to guard against it.

It's not until the last ten minutes of the movie that there is a sudden shift, an unveiling. The entire movie changes and gets turned upside down.

You thought you were watching a certain kind of movie, with a particular set of characters with specific motivations dealing with unique circumstances and leading to a particular possible outcome. When in fact it wasn't that at all. There's a plot twist.

The new information pulled back the curtain to reveal what was previously unknown. The new information then changes everything about the story, characters, and circumstances up to that point.

So now when you go back and watch the movie again with the information from the end, you begin to see and understand the story at an entirely new level.

This is precisely one way the Bible is written and should be understood.

When Jesus is on the road to Emmaus and explains to the disciples walking with Him how all of the Old Testament is leading to and about

Him, it's the same point about the entirety of Scripture being a single unit. There is an overarching theme and plot line.

The apostles, after Jesus ascended and they are filled with the Holy Spirit, preached and explained how everything God was doing up to that point was about bringing Jesus into history to die and resurrect.

The book of Hebrews goes into significant detail to make the point that what God was doing with all of the particulars of the law, tradition, journey, Israel, kings, prophets, and priests in the Old Testament was unfolding a story that had Jesus as the main character.

When Paul is discussing marriage in his letters in the New Testament and saying that the great mystery is now being revealed, it is exactly what happens in the last ten minutes of *The Village*. The veil is pulled back and you are clued into what is really happening in the story.

Understanding that the gospel was the center, Jesus was the center of the gospel, and the entire Scripture narrative was unified, helped me to begin to see how all of the varying pieces, themes, genres, concepts, events, and characters were coming together to form one explanation of things.

The second element that I began to give attention to was God as a Trinity. It seemed to be central to who God was and how He operated. Being a trinity wasn't just another item on a list of characteristics about God but appeared to be near or at the center of who He was and brought all the other characteristics together.

A friend I was interacting with at the time shared that God being in three persons is perfectly in line with the way the cosmos and humanity functions. God could not and would not create in the fashion that He did if he was not three persons. A unitary God would have no purpose, no glory, and probably no means of creating anything outside of Himself, let alone people, if there was no relational element in Himself first.

This began to make sense as I thought about how the central elements of what God has created and what He was doing in history were things like union, love, and relationship.

If these things, initiated by God, were not ultimately and primarily rooted in who and what God was in the first place, then they could not be ultimate or significant. This deserves its own time and study but let me leave you with some excerpts from an explanation from Abdu Murray in a Question-and-Answer session.

Murray mentions that there are three levels to handle the legitimacy of the trinity: the logical possibility, the Biblical warranting, and the Theological necessity of the Trinity. The third one was where I spent the most time processing. Here is how he explains.

> When there were no other beings than God, then who was He relating to, before He created us and the angels and all these things? He needed to create something outside of Himself in order to be a relatable or relational being. Because you don't just love in a vacuum. You have to love someone or something. You have to be merciful and compassionate to someone or something. So, God would have had to create something outside of Himself to be a relational being. The Problem with that is, if God needs something outside of Himself then He can't be fully great. The Trinity solves the problem. It doesn't create a problem. It solves it beautifully because God doesn't need anything outside of Himself to be a relational being. The Father loves the Son. The Son loves the Spirit. The Spirit loves the Father and the Son. And on it goes in eternity, in the community of the Trinity. He never lacks relationship. He defines relationship. And therefore, He is a Great God. RZIM HQ "Is the Trinity A Contradiction? Abdu Murray Q&A RZIM," YouTube, April 6, 2020, 11:20.
>
> https://youtu.be/xYFSN-Ix7iE

5
My Political Awakening

I couldn't care less about politics. Growing up, my dad was into politics and was always up to speed on what was happening on the national, state, and local levels. Living in Chicago, the politics were certainly something to be concerned about.

But me? I just didn't care. The reason was, I didn't understand. There was just no place in my conceptual framework for the political domain. But that was about to change.

I came across a *New York Times* bestselling author, Eric Metaxas, and a series he hosts titled, "Socrates in the City." In this series, Eric hosts influential figures from a wide spectrum of fields including scientists, politicians, philosophers, and writers.

One guest in particular, Os Guinness, piqued my interest. He discussed the current political state from a philosophical framework that was rooted theologically. It wasn't the typical evangelical talking points that I and so many were so accustomed to.

It became clear, as I listened, that politics was nested inside philosophical ideas. Dr. Guinness was able to unpack some of those ideas. This helped me get a handle on why politics was such a big deal.

Around the same time, I came across people like Ben Shapiro, Andrew Klavan, Thomas Sowell, and Dave Rubin. Each was interested in politics but were able to bring context to the discussion that pulled back the veil to show more of what was behind and underneath the issues.

In this information age and era of social media, it became apparent that memes, paragraph posts, and three-minute videos on some of the most controversial topics are what dominated. Quite a significant problem. The opposite was needed.

Finding the places where topics were given more time and space to be explored, discussed, and argued over seemed to be a far more beneficial means in learning, understanding, and pursuing truth.

Politics, at least in the American context, was predominantly divided between conservative and liberal. Of all possible values and ways of dividing, why was it split up in this way?

I began to think about what each of those two opposite values meant independently and in relation to one another. At the same time, I was listening to voices who helped me see the philosophy underneath which the politics stood.

One of the most significant problems in our political arena and in the public square today is the absence of philosophical understanding upon which our politics rest.

What is the value of liberalism? Not politically, just the concept of being liberal all by itself. There is a priority there that is so fundamental to being human, to surviving and thriving, that it's no wonder that it is of highest value for an entire society.

The same could be said for the concept of being conservative.

We each have a core need to be open and grow. In order to do that, we have to be creative and experimental; willing to take risks. If we stay put, we become stagnant.

We have a fundamental need to be secure, protected, strong, tested, and sure. In order to maintain that, we have to be calculated, disciplined, and goal oriented.

How fundamental are these two aspects of reality? Why are they the basic division in the political domain? What were they rooted in?

I grew up hearing and understanding that theology was the root and foundation of all fields of study. I knew if I wanted to understand the political or the philosophical, I had to dig deeper and see how they were rooted theologically.

The problem for most people, certainly in the Christian domain today, is they don't understand how differing fields of study are related to one another and can't or shouldn't be skipped over in trying to gain understanding.

So many Christians will try to tie their political arguments down to theology without understanding the philosophical concepts, ideas, and values that the politics are directly tied to. They just end up with extremely weak thoughts and arguments, even while using the Bible.

Marxism, Capitalism, Socialism, Communism, Individualism, Postmodernism are value systems. They are worldviews. They are frameworks for how we see and organize as a society. They are philosophical ideas.

There are reasons why they resonate with a particular group of people or one side of the political aisle at any given time.

Listening to people who discussed the ideas and values underneath the politics is when my eyes were opened to what the big deal about politics was.

But the ideas and values and concepts underneath the politics were not hanging in mid-air either. They weren't arbitrary. They resonated with humans at a very significant level. So where were they coming from, and what gave them such power and meaning?

6
Truth: Round One

My journey continued. I wanted to know and understand why things were the way they were, the good, the bad, and the ugly. At the same time, I was trying to figure out who I was and why I was the way I am.

There was no indication that with all the analyzing that I would find anything of deep significance. All I knew was that what I had sorted out to this point was correct.

Learning to be critical in order to find what was true was not just in line with the central theme of Christianity, but also with the function of the cosmos.

Even while believing I was on the right track it always wasn't so obvious. On track to where?

The deeper I delved into concepts and myself the riskier it became. There was no indication that a destination of overall explanation was any closer. Was I wasting time analyzing and critiquing?

There were three things that stood out as I continued to explore: The first was the concept of ***God's sovereignty***.

> In Christian doctrine, God is in control of all. That went right along with my personality and tendency to be more passive. I had good reason theologically not to exert myself if I was uncertain, which was a lot of the time. If everything is in God's control and nothing will be able to change His plan or will, then I can be content.
>
> I was a strong believer in the sovereignty of God, but I was using it almost as a crutch. I was using it as an excuse to cover

my weaknesses and fears, as well as support my reserved tendencies.

The second concept was *meaning*.

I learned early on that everything is meaningful. The cosmos and all details, great or small, are not arbitrary. The meaning is present in part because everything is connected and rooted to something actual and eternal.

If you pushed the atheistic worldview to its bottom, required it to be consistent, it would be true to say that nothing has meaning. Even attempting to argue against that point would be as significant as stating whatever "gibberish" amounted to.

Although I knew that there was meaning in different positions people were in and ways they were doing things, it wasn't obvious why my position or approach was less meaningful or significant. Where I was, seemed just as good a place as any to sort things out.

The third was the concept of *infinitude*.

One thing I realized was true and true about my thought life was that options in perspective were boundless.

Why would one way of viewing something be selected over an infinite number of others when many of them were seemingly just as viable?

This seemed to slow me down constantly in thought, in will, and in action. When trying to pursue what is good or best or preferable, facing a reality of infinite options was a reasonable obstacle.

Those three concepts: God's ultimate control, meaning, and infinitude began to validate me in my personality. At the same time, they became barriers to my need for growth, development, and movement forward.

While in the middle of my personal journey of listening and learning, I began to notice all of the back and forth happening on social media in and around politics.

It became apparent that, as many posts came out in support of a particular view on an issue, there were just as many reasonable posts with an opposing view. What did that mean? How could that be?

If truth was something actual and real, then how was it able to navigate through the amount of information that wasn't just nuanced, but seemingly opposite in nature?

It seemed that everyone, no matter their view, had some degree of accurate info and was claiming to possess the truth. If everyone, holding differing and opposing views was claiming to have the truth, then the truth couldn't be identified simply by who claimed it and had reason to back it up. Because everyone was playing that card.

Everyone claimed to have the truth. No matter what side or subject matter; religious, philosophical, political, scientific, personal, and so on, the arguments always came down to figuring out who had the truth. But that only seemed to be the issue at the surface.

Underneath, the real issue and question was, what is truth?

That became my next quest. I had to sort out the nature of truth. Before anyone could figure out who had it, we had to figure out what it was.

If I have it, how do I know I have it?

What I did figure out is that in order for truth to be what it is, it had to possess and be in relationship with some very specific properties.

For example,

> Truth had to be eternal. If it's not eternal, then it's just a conceptual mirage. Given enough time it would change or cease to be.
>
> Truth had to be in union with all power. If it wasn't, then it could be changed by a greater force and it would no longer be what it is.
>
> Truth had to be connected to all knowledge. If it wasn't, then the possibility of something that wasn't known could inform and change what it had already calculated. It would cease to hold its position as the ultimate standard in relation to knowledge and information.
>
> Truth had to be all good, connected to the source and originating properties that make up what goodness is. If it wasn't good at any point, no matter how minute, then it would not be trustworthy.

That was a decent start. It made sense. It also was in perfect alignment with what the Christian worldview stated about truth's relationship to God. However, it still didn't seem to bring forth an image or a clarity of description in the mind. It still seemed evasive, foggy, and formless.

I'll never forget the day I pulled out my phone and typed into the google search engine, "What is truth?"

I scrolled over the first few options and then came across a YouTube video. It was a podcast between popular atheist Sam Harris and a guy by the name of Jordan Peterson.

> I knew little to nothing about who Jordan Peterson was. I knew Sam Harris from many of the debates on atheism. I

had no idea that the conversation between these two was going to be one of the most profound conversations I'd ever encountered.

"Waking Up with Sam Harris Podcast #62 w Jordan Peterson"
https://youtu.be/2lO6WJ9rfs4

Because I heard Sam Harris's debates with Christians on the existence of God, to hear his thoughts and arguments for the concept of truth was fascinating. The conversation is over two hours long.

You have to understand, I grew up in a religious culture where the nature of truth was primary and central. I had certainly heard definitions of truth. But here was a conversation between two modern elite thinkers who understood the significance of the subject. I knew that all roads lead to this point.

So, when I began to listen, I was listening with intent. I was considering everything I had ever heard, learned, and had figured out to this point. I knew that I could not move forward without first sorting out the nature of truth.

I was absolutely stunned by what was described in this conversation.

Just weeks before finding this podcast, as I mentioned above, I realized that knowledge and information are infinite. There is no thing in which all information is known about it. There is always more. You cannot exhaust information.

If that is correct, then what does that mean about what truth is and what is understood to be true?

In this conversation between Harris and Peterson, they appeared to be taking two different stances on the definition of truth.

Sam Harris took the position of truth being absolute and definitive. He sounded more like a fundamentalist Christian than an atheist, but that's beside the point. Truth, according to Harris, was something that was objective, unchanging, secure and could be held to as tightly as anything.

Peterson seemed to understand that aspect and point, emphasized by Harris. However, he was trying to highlight another aspect of truth. Namely, that it had to contend with the unknown. Whatever truth you possessed in knowledge, there was always more to be gained. The claim to have the truth, then, meant that you had it in part.

This went right in line with what I had understood about knowledge and information. It also resonated with the concept of God in the Bible.

God is infinite. We will always be pursuing Him in knowledge and satisfaction. There is never a point where we will reach the end of who God is.

In the Christian explanation of things, truth finds its identity all wrapped up in who and what God is. God being infinite certainly comes to play in the makeup of what truth is.

Truth wasn't just a defining, strict, closed, sealed standard. It was simultaneously open, continuous, boundless, and infinite. This, this, THIS was a significant discovery!

Truth itself is a paradox!

Paradox wasn't just a small glitch in God's system—quite the contrary. It was central to the entire design.

7
The Arrival

While delving deeper into theology, philosophy, and politics, again I was also trying to sort myself out. Was there something in those fields of study that could give me some insight into my own weaknesses?

After following some of the controversy that threw professor Dr. Jordan Peterson onto the public scene, I began to listen through his lectures. He posted on YouTube just about all of the university course content that he taught. This would prove to be quite insightful.

The more I learned about myself the more I saw the reason why I wasn't so abnormal. There was a reason to double down in my personality tendencies, which included being analytical and idealistic.

However, it wasn't working. It wasn't enough, and I knew it. But I didn't know what I needed. What was I missing? Where was I wrong?

I'll never forget the moment I heard it. It was exactly what I needed. It was the answer I had been searching for. It was the cure, the truth.

I knew it was true, and the truth I needed because it affirmed me as strongly as I have ever been affirmed. Simultaneously it exposed and implicated me as accurately and effectively as I ever have been.

I was on the stairwell, sweeping as I had done countless times before on the job.

On those steps, with a broom or a mop in my hand, having gone up and down, from floor to floor, running or walking, I spent hours upon hours listening and searching. There were music, sermons, lectures, debates, conversations, podcasts and yet no guarantee that any of it would lead to anywhere better than where I was or had been.

But this particular morning, I was listening through the "2017 Maps of Meaning" lecture series by Jordan Peterson.

In this lecture he was explaining that at the bottom of reality is order. Order is the known. It's what's defined, bordered and safe. It's routine, structure, tradition, or hierarchy. It's the walled city, the state, the institution, or the paradisal garden. There is nothing beneath it. It is the highest value.

That resonated with me. It was describing me; my personality, my value system, my needs, my make up.

However, that value and bedrock of order was not alone. It was shared by two others. Two that were just as significant. One was the opposite. It was a reality defined by chaos.

Chaos is the unknown, unformed, boundless, open, free, or infinite. It's a threat and uncertainty. It's the wilderness and what's foreign.

The third could be described as the proper mode of being. It's positioned in between the other two bedrock realities. It's the tension and contending between the two.

So, the tendency was to favor one side and shy away from the other. Being able to only recognize the benefit of one and only see the downside of the other. This described me.

Yet the right way was to value both. The correct way was to be subject to the known and order, but to also see its limitation and to move into the unknown and pursue the infinite.

It wasn't enough to just be okay with my opposite, but to value disorder, uncertainty, and failure because that is the only path forward. There is no way to be alive, living, growing, developing and accepting of eternal life without stepping toward that reality.

Peterson states that most often the answer we need is in the place we least want to look.

> Every new frontier that can be conquered is an advance forward and there is no shortage of frontier because we're surrounded by the unknown. We're surrounded by our own ignorance and we can continually move into that domain, into the domain of chaos. Or we can restructure pathological

order. And that's the secret to proper being.—Jordan B. Peterson "Lecture Biblical Series VII: Walking with God: Noah and the Flood" YouTube video, July 18, 2017, 2:32:20. https://youtu.be/6gFjB9FTN58

That was it. I wanted all reality to be contained in the domain of the known. I needed everything structured and in order. But it wasn't. The difference between what was inside the structure and out, was not the line of morality or goodness.

The unknown, unformed, not yet frontier, was just as good, just as valuable, just as needed to be had than the known, orderly, structured hierarchy. That was the answer I needed, the one I had been looking for, for years.

At the same time, it was the answer I had been running from, the one I had decided was the enemy, the answer that I was terrified of. But it was the truth, And I knew it.

I had spent most of my life, and certainly the last twelve years, building into my theology and framework of reality, with doctrine, ideas, and facts that truth itself was contained in order, structure, and the known. But now, this new huge light bulb moment completely transformed, challenged, and updated my framework of what true and good reality was.

I had one question left. If this updated framework of order and chaos, known and unknown, conservative and liberal, home and frontier was correct, how was it rooted in what I knew was the source of all reality, God Himself?

I knew and believed that God was real. I also knew that central to his nature was Him being infinite.

Having been given eternal life by Him meant, in part, Him being the main attraction in all of reality and that we would never reach the end of Him. We would always be searching Him, enjoying Him, pursuing Him, all the while knowing Him and actually relating to Him.

God is infinite and knowable at every point.

I came across Francis Schaeffer's book *Escape from Reason*.

There were two paragraphs in the second chapter, and when I read them, I knew I hit the bottom.

Up to this point, it had been like traveling deeper and deeper into a cave that became more and more narrow, darker with every step. The walk became a crawl, and just when I thought it would come to a dead end, there was a huge opening. An opening that led into a large space, like an old Gothic cathedral. There in the center was a huge structure, like a sculpture that had as its form the definition of all reality.

It was like reaching the lowest point of the bottom of the ocean floor. Everything was built and resting on it. It was the core of the earth. Everything came from and was built on this.

The two paragraphs read;

> It is an important principle to remember, in the contemporary interest in communication and in language study, that the biblical presentation is that, though we do not have exhaustive truth, we have from the Bible what I term "true truth." In this way we know true truth about God, true truth about man and something truly about nature. Thus, on the basis of the Scriptures, while we do not have exhaustive knowledge, we have true and unified knowledge.
>
> We must now see something else about man. To do this we must notice that everything in the biblical system goes back to God. I love the biblical system as a system. While we might not like the connotation of the word system, because it sounds rather cold, this does not mean that the biblical teaching is not a system. Everything goes back to the beginning and thus the system has a unique beauty and perfection because everything is under the apex of the whole, and everything flows from this in a non-contradictory way. The Bible says God is a living God and it tells us much about Him, but, most significantly perhaps, for twentieth-century man, it speaks of Him as both a personal God and an infinite God. This is the kind of God who is 'there,' who exists. Furthermore, this is the only system, the only religion, that has this kind of God. The gods of the East are infinite by definition, in the sense that they encompass all—the evil as well as the good— but they are not personal. The gods of the West were

personal, but they were very limited. The Teutonic, the Roman and the Greek gods were all the same—personal but not infinite. The Christian God, the God of the Bible, is personal-infinite.—Francis Scheaffer, *Escape From Reason* (Downers Grove, Illinois: InterVarsity Press, 1968), 21, 25.

Reading those paragraphs while listening through Jordan Peterson's lectures through Genesis and his "Maps of Meaning" lectures in which he describes the bottom of all reality as order and potential, known and unknown, structure and infinitude was nothing short of mind-blowing.

Peterson describes the God in the Bible in terms of a trinity and breaks down the differences between them with the framework of order, chaos and a mediating entity.

So, when I read Schaeffer's statements, everything clicked!

The framework of all of reality at every level in the most fundamental sense matched the definition of who and what God is.

How or why would it be any other way?

The problem isn't that we don't see the pattern all around us in varying fields of study or in life, but we don't recognize it across fields being the same pattern. Most importantly, we don't see that it's the pattern that describes who God is in the most fundamental and profound sense.

From the moment I read those two paragraphs by Schaeffer, I began having several epiphanies every day for about the next month and a half. I was experiencing what I can only describe as something like a psychological nirvana. I could not believe what I had discovered. The thoughts of explanation and understanding that were forming were exploding like fireworks in my mind.

They have slowed down since then, but they haven't stopped.

This writing project is simply an attempt to sketch out that most fundamental framework of reality coming from the most basic outline of who God is and how He functions. It sketches out how He has created and acted in the world as well as how He as explained and revealed Himself in the Bible.

The singularity of reality is the framework found in the three-person Godhead of the Bible:

it's structure, openness, and mediation. In Francis Schaeffer's words, it's the personal-infinite God.

How could the most important doctrine of God—the Trinity—at the same time be the most elusive, least understood, and seemingly irrelevant? Pause and think about that.

This is God, the triune being of the Bible. The source and framework of the gospel, and all things.

THE HOLY SPIRIT: A SNAPSHOT
What came first, the chicken or the egg?

8
An Introduction

> If somebody tells you that there's a rule, break it. That's the only thing that moves things forward.—Hans Zimmer, G.O.A.T. UniVerseCity, "Hans Zimmer Teaches Film Scoring | Official Trailer | MasterClass, YouTube Video, 4:07, November 15, 2023. https://youtu.be/bdC3zFuVvGs?si=9gggB0OxkN8pOUcW

I sat down at the baby grand piano, as I often do, to bang out a few chord progressions. I wanted to see if by some magical means, I had the mastery of gliding over the keys, stretching and arriving at new destinations of beauty and adventure.

But my clunky, short fingered hands only fell on the keys to produce the rehearsed routine notes that I was familiar with.

In this case, a particular melody came to mind. It was one that I had learned previously and now wanted to recall and tap out in hopes to show that my melodious endeavors were not completely in vain.

The frustration began to rise as I attempted to recall and play the song. I found nothing but fumbling fingers and odd chaotic notes. For the moment, it ironically mirrored where I was.

> Listen to my prayer, O God, and hide not yourself from my supplication!
>
> Attend to me and answer me; I am restless and distraught in my complaint and must moan.
>
> My heart is grievously pained with in me, and the terrors of death have fallen upon me.
>
> Fear and trembling have come upon me; horror and fright have overwhelmed me.
>
> And I say, Oh, that I had wings like a dove! I would fly away and be at rest.

40

PARADOX LOST

Yes, I would wander far away, I would lodge in the wilderness. I would hasten to escape

And to find a shelter from the stormy wind and tempest.—Psalm 55:1–8 (ampc)

• • • •

I RETURNED HOME FROM school out of state some years ago. I had taken notice, even before returning, that my home church was struggling. Spirits were strained and things began to become unsettled. With a lack of clear direction, myself, I reverted back to what I was most certain of. That was stepping in near the center of the church organization, and as best I could, lift with what knowledge, skill, and enthusiasm I had to help carry the spiritual project forward.

It did not take long to realize that what I experienced felt more like a heavy dead weight that didn't seem to be moving in any particular positive direction.

So, there I stood. It was dark. Despite the effort and energy to usher in light, it grew darker still. Like black clouds rolling in from a pending storm.

Maybe it was just me. Or perhaps what I was sensing was a reflection back into my own soul. Or was it something larger happening in society? If I sorted out the darkness in myself, would I be able to implement the aid to the darkness outside?

I was the music/worship leader at church. We had rehearsal on Saturday mornings.

On my way home from work throughout the week, I would often stop at the store to pick up some snacks to enjoy for the weekend.

This particular Friday evening, I found myself navigating through the candy aisle, trying to find something new. I reached out and snagged a bag of dark chocolate candies.

That night and into Saturday morning, before rehearsal, I was thinking about something I learned that week. I was debating in my mind whether I should share it with the music team in our rehearsal.

I had been listening through a lecture series, "Maps of Meaning" by Jordan Peterson, a seasoned clinical psychologist and tenured professor of psychology.

At a certain section of the course, he had been expositing the Disney movie *Pinocchio*. He was discussing its meaning scene by scene. He reached the section near the beginning of the movie when the evening ends and a new day begins.

The scene depicts a blue sky and doves flying.

He mentions that the doves signify the fresh start, a new beginning.

He references how the Holy Spirit is signified by a dove in biblical stories for the same purpose. He continues and states that it is just like the scene pictured at the baptism of Jesus. The dove comes down and hovers over Jesus, symbolizing and signaling that something new has arrived. It's the dawn of a new age.

Immediately following his reference, I had a progression of thoughts.

The first was, that seems to be precisely what is happening at the end of the flood story in Genesis when Noah sends out the dove. There is a storm, a flood, judgment, death, and the end of an age. Then, once the storm completes its task, the dove comes on the scene.

The dove flies over the water and finds the place where the future can be had and lived in, beyond judgment and darkness. The dove signifies and shows the place where there is promise and hope for a new beginning.

The next thought was, that is exactly what occurred on the day of Pentecost. Once Jesus completed the journey through judgement and suffering, He resurrected from the dead.

As He left, it was the Holy Spirit who came onto the scene, signifying the dawn of a new era.

Then, my next thought was, and that's what is described as happening with every converted individual, from the time of Pentecost forward. The Holy Spirit is given to the person who identifies as one deserving to be rightly judged, punished, and aligned with Jesus, claiming Him as their substitute. The Holy Spirit marks them as one who has passed through judgment and brought out in new life, signifying rebirth, a fresh beginning, a hope of future.

We see the same theme on display given in the opening lines of the entire Scripture narrative.

> The earth was without form and an empty waste, and darkness was upon the face of the very great deep. The Spirit of God was moving (hovering, brooding) over the face of the waters.—Genesis 1:2 (ampc)

The picture in this passage is describing a bird hovering over the barren, chaotic deep. It's seemingly showing us again the role of the Spirit in relation to the new or just birthed.

Between all of these images, there is a recurring theme.

There's darkness, water, and the unformed unknown. Then, not avoidance, but movement toward and into it, and coming out of it. The Holy Spirit then arrives, marking that new territory/place/person, as the beginning, the place where life will continue into the future.

So, I woke up Saturday morning. I had just a few moments between getting out of bed and making my way to rehearsal to decide if I should share with the music team what I had been thinking about.

I was shifting back and forth in my mind as I finished up my morning routine. I thought to bring the rest of the chocolate candies I had bought the night before to share with the team. I walked over to the table to pick up the bag of candy. In an instant, I was struck by what I saw! There, sat the bag of chocolate . . . Dove chocolate candies!

As I passed the bag around the circle to the band members, I shared with them what seemed to be a clear description of a significant role that was unique to the Holy Spirit.

But that was just the beginning.

9
Genesis 1:2

Why a dove or a bird?
In the opening lines of the Bible there is a depiction that is extremely chaotic and frightening. The second line in the entire Bible begins,

> The earth was without form and an empty waste, and darkness was upon the face of the very great deep. The Spirit of God was moving (hovering, brooding) over the face of the waters (Genesis 1:2 ampc).

This verse sits in between such power and goodness. Verse 1 is incredible. Verse 3 launches us on an amazing adventure. But what are we to make of these lines in verse 2?

This description doesn't seem to fit. It appears out of place. It does not seem to coincide with the God we have formulated in our modern mind. There is a huge sense of mystery. Why this deep, dark valley right here at the outset of it all?

"Without form"—No shape. No structure. No organization. No system. No place. No path. No rules or framework. Unrelatable. How should you act? What should you feel?

There's dysfunction and no meaning. It's chaos. The term "water" is used at the end of the verse, giving us a depiction of what this open chaos is like. Water is fluid, formless. It's level. Equality means things are at the same level.

Water is also open. Because there is no path or set aim or structure, infinite reigns. The options and potential are limitless. The possibilities are endless.

"An empty waste"—Useless. Hollow. Unproductive. Desert. Barren. Nothing beneficial being produced. No fruit. No future.

A theme that runs through the Scriptures narrative is that of the barren woman, the barren womb. There is Sarai, Rebekah, Rachel, Manoah's wife, Hannah, and Elizabeth. What's ironic is this theme is at the heart of the promise that God would provide a child that would be the Savior of the world.

"Darkness was upon the face of the very great deep"—Not just deep. Great deep. Very great deep. It's unsearchable. Unknowable. Not only is it the very great deep, but to make matters worse, darkness covers it. There is no sense of perception or direction.

What lurks in the very great deep is unknown and has potential to pull you down. There is real threat present.

These lines are extremely overwhelming. The threat of being consumed, overtaken, devoured by this element of reality is as sure as anything. We feel this threat on any given day in any given situation. It's real, and it happens to us and those around us all the time.

The open, chaotic, unformed, unknown, infinite can consume us, and it does.

Natural disasters, illness, divorce, tragedy, rejection, violence, abuse, unemployment, pain, and death.

Is the unformed, empty waste, the very great deep and the infinite only negative? No. It seems to just be a fundamental fact about reality. The infinite is potential. Anything is possible.

How do we avoid being devoured by the threats inside infinitude and manage to continue safely?

The second part of the verse states, "The Spirit of God was moving (hovering, brooding) over the face of the waters."

It's the Spirit. That title alone gives us an indication of the lack of form. Spirit is not concrete. Its fluid.

"Moving, hovering"—The Spirit is described as functioning and operating in a way that is unique and different from the other two persons of the Trinity. The Spirit is operating like a bird.

Consider that term "hovering." We are familiar with this imagery. We have seen drones, helicopters, and eagles. They are up in the air, able to have a view and perspective that could not be reached if on the ground.

It's the helicopter flying over the natural disaster, like a town destroyed by a tornado, earthquake, or flood.

The helicopter is flying over and assessing the situation. It's directing aid. What's beneath is too chaotic. It's impassible from the surface. The helicopter, the bird, the Spirit is able to move over, see and assist from its position.

This is precisely the image we are given in the Noah flood story when he sends out the bird once the ark rests in place.

"Brooding"—This means for a mother bird to sit on and cover her eggs. It also means to contemplate or to think about something in dissatisfaction. There is a sense of dissatisfaction. Things are not complete.

Also, there is intentional presence and activity to bring about something that is beneficial.

With the Spirit of God present, what comes out of the depths of the chaotic waters is able to be nurtured and cared for, leading to growth and maturity.

The Spirit is the entity uniquely characterized by and equipped to contend with that which is open, infinite, formless, and unknown. He is able to produce that which can live. Psalms 139 displays this well.

10
Freedom and Energy

Birds have wings. They are free. They display, in real time and space, what it is to be boundless. They have the ability to fly and be open without restriction. It's a demonstration that there is a downside to limitation and benefit to infinity and beyond.

Speaking of infinity and beyond, take Woody and Buzz Lightyear from the movie *Toy Story* as an example.

Woody is a cowboy: the traditional, dependable, loyal, faithful, toy. Buzz Lightyear is the new, fresh, latest, and most recently developed technology toy. He's a space traveler who has wings! Both Woody and Buzz play out their unique roles, giving us a story of how central this theme is.

God is an infinite being. He's boundless, without parameters. He has no defining lines, no barriers, no borders. How do you relate to an infinite being? In a simple expression, you are never through. New, fresh, beginning, genesis will always be a part of the experience when relating to this God.

When you are free, you are unrestricted. The options and possibilities are extended. Limits are left behind. Venturing out is of highest value. If God is infinite, and all that He is is good, then never being stuck, or stopping, and always moving forward, is a fundamental element. It's bedrock, the bottom of reality.

"But their minds were hardened. For to this day, at the reading of the old covenant, the same veil remains; it is not lifted, because it is set aside only in Christ. Yet still today, whenever Moses is read, a veil lies over their hearts, but whenever a person turns to the Lord, the veil is removed. Now the Lord is the Spirit, and where the Spirit of the Lord is, there is freedom."—2 Corinthians 3:14–17 (CSB)

God is giving us a description of Himself and how he functions and operates, not just in our reality created, but in his own nature.

Not only is freedom uniquely associated with the Holy Spirit, but power also. There is an energy that enables significant movement, navigation and change.

Where did Samson, son of the once barren woman Manoah's wife and known as the strongest man to ever live, get his strength? Did he get it from the length of his hair?

> Judges 13:24-25—So the woman gave [in due time] birth to a son and named him Samson; and the boy grew, and the Lord blessed him. And the Spirit of the Lord began to stir him at times in Mahaneh Dan, between Zorah and Eshtaol.
>
> 14:5-6—Then Samson went down to Timnah with his father and mother [to arrange the marriage], and they came as far as the vineyards of Timnah; and suddenly, a young lion came roaring toward him. The Spirit of the Lord came upon him mightily, and he tore the lion apart as one tears apart a young goat, and he had nothing at all in his hand . . .
>
> 14:19—Then the Spirit of the Lord came upon him mightily, and he went down to Ashkelon and killed thirty of them and took their gear, and gave changes of clothes to those who had explained the riddle.
>
> 15:14-15—When he came to Lehi, the Philistines came shouting to meet him. And the Spirit of the Lord came upon him mightily, and the ropes on his arms were like flax (linen) that had been burned, and his bonds dropped off his hands. He found a fresh jawbone of a donkey, so he reached out his hand and took it and killed a thousand men with it.—(amp)

You get the point.

"Not by might, nor by power, but by My Spirit."—Zechariah 4:6 (amp)

Jesus, after his resurrection, states to his disciples, "Listen carefully: I am sending the promise of My Father [the Holy Spirit] upon you; but you are to remain in the city [of Jerusalem] until you are clothed (fully equipped) with power from on high."—Luke 24:49 (amp)

At the beginning of the book of Acts, it introduces us to the Holy Spirit. It does so in a moment that follows the long tradition and law of the Old Testament and even more recently, the life, death and resurrection of Jesus.

He's introduced with these words by Jesus, "You will receive power and ability when the Holy Spirit comes upon you; and you will be my witnesses [to tell people about me] both in Jerusalem and in all Judea, and Samaria, and even to the ends of the Earth.—Acts 1:8 (AMP)

"And if the Spirit of Him who raised Jesus from the dead lives in you, He who raised Christ Jesus from the dead will also give life to your mortal bodies through His Spirit, who lives in you."—Romans 8:11 (AMP)

"I pray that the eyes of your heart may be enlightened in order that you may know the hope to which he has called you, the riches of his glorious inheritance in his holy people, and his incomparably great power for us who believe. That power is the same as the mighty strength he exerted when he raised Christ from the dead . . ."—Ephesians 1:18–20a (NIV)

"May the God of hope fill you with all joy and peace in believing [through the experience of your faith] that by the power of the Holy Spirit you will abound in hope and overflow with confidence in His promises."— Romans 15:13 (AMP)

"For I will not [even] presume to speak of anything except what Christ has done through me [as an instrument in His hands], resulting in the obedience of the Gentiles [to the gospel], by word and deed, with the power of signs and wonders, [and all of it] in the power of the Spirit."—Romans 15:18–19 (AMP)

After centuries of law, confinement for the sake of holiness, patriarchy, and tradition, God the Son arrives embodied, in flesh. Once the Son ascends back to the Father, the Holy Spirit comes to center stage. He brings an energy that leads to an explosion that we are still feeling today.

The nature of power and freedom being fundamental to reality is only valuable or necessary if action is of value. Action is only of value if the infinite is a fundamental reality. Otherwise, why act? Why change?

This energy is what the Holy Spirit brings on the historical scale, the spiritual scale, the personal scale. It's His fundamental nature and how He functions. He is the power and the energy.

11
Experiment and Explore

Freedom and Energy means the drive to experiment and explore. The Holy Spirit is about the new and fresh. He's analogous to innovation. He pushes past the current boundaries and moves beyond the tradition. There is always more.

God is infinite. For Him to be glorified maximally by finite creatures, He has to always be prompting them beyond where they currently are.

That seems to be exactly what we see when the Holy Spirit is on the scene in the Scripture storyline.

We see it in Genesis 1:2, the flood story, Jesus' baptism, Pentecost in Acts, the conversion of the sinner to Christian, and so on. He's showing up at the point of transition and helping move things from old to new.

After the waters cover the face of the earth and the ark rests on the mountain, the story describes Noah sending out a bird a few times to navigate and explore the unknown. It doesn't happen in one shot. There is trial and trying.

Jonah gets called by God to go to the foreign city to bring the news of salvation. Jonah ends up almost drowning in the sea and gets carried and saved by the fish. He then is spit up on dry land safely and eventually makes his way to the morally barren city. Jonah's name means "Dove."

When God's chosen people are enslaved in Egypt, God leads them out. But not directly into the promised land. He leads them into the wasteland, the wilderness, the barren desert.

When Jesus begins His ministry, He walks out of the waters and is led BY THE SPIRIT into the wilderness. It's there that He comes face to face with the serpent, the monster of the wasteland. He is offered a few different options to choose from as means to move forward. In His first letter to the church in Corinth, Paul states,

> For God has unveiled them and revealed them to us through the [Holy] Spirit; for the Spirit searches all things [diligently], even [sounding and measuring] the [profound] depths of God [the divine counsels and things far beyond human understanding]. For what person knows the thoughts and motives of a man except the man's spirit within him? So also no one knows the thoughts of God except the Spirit God. Now we have received, not the spirit of the world, but the [Holy] Spirit who is from God, so that we may know and understand the [wonderful] things freely give to us by God. We also speak of these things, not in words taught or supplied by human wisdom, but in those taught by the Spirit, combining and interpreting spiritual with spiritual words [for those being guided by the Holy Spirit].—1 Corinthians 2:10–13 (amp)

The Holy Spirit brings a power to break free and then the ability to navigate in and through new, uncharted and often dangerous territory.

The Holy Spirit is the first on the scene, like a first responder. He is fit to fly over, navigate through, lead and direct to the next good place.

We see Him in the picture of creation, in Genesis 1:2, hovering over the water. Then there's the description of the dove at the end of Noah's flood. Then the scene at the conclusion of Jesus' baptism, when He leads Him into the wilderness. There is the explanation of the ascending, crucified and resurrected Jesus, sending the Holy Spirit to His followers; in order to move them forward into the future. Out of their promised borders, and into the land of the foreigner to establish an assembly of people from every nation.

When the nation of Israel escaped from slavery in Egypt, they ended up in the desert, trusting the promise of God to provide a new land for them to live in. God instructed Moses to send spies into this new land that was inhabited by other people. When the spies returned to report what they witnessed, they came back carrying a branch with a single cluster of grapes (Numbers 13), just like the dove sent out of the ark returning with an olive branch in its beak, giving a sign to Noah.

When the spies reported, all but two were pessimistic. Caleb and Joshua were optimistic. They were enthusiastic and confident that God's people could move into the land and conquer in the face of any giant or obstacle. This is precisely how the Holy Spirit functions.

The Spirit over the waters in Genesis 1:2.

The dove over the waters after the flood.

The dreamer, Joseph, with his colorful coat, the first into Egypt before saving his family from the famine.

Caleb and Joshua, spying out the promised land and reporting optimistically.

John the Baptist, a master of water, living in the wilderness, precedes the Savior of the world.

The Holy Spirit as a dove, hovering over Jesus in the baptismal waters.

The Holy Spirit leading Jesus, after His baptism, into the wilderness.

The Holy Spirit, falling with power, on the followers of Jesus after His ascension into heaven.

At one point, I was explaining to a friend the definitions and functions between the persons of the Trinity and describing how they showed up in the baptism of Jesus. My friend stated that typically the only point made about the trinity in relation to the story of Jesus' baptism, is that there is a Trinity.

There is little to no development of understanding and explanation of how the persons in the Trinity operate uniquely and in relation to one another.

12
Reproduction and Multiplication

Let's take a closer look at the term "brooding" in Genesis 1:2. There is a picture of a bird hovering over its nest of offspring, hinting at the element of reproduction.

Reproduction is bringing into being a copy or representation of something already in existence. It's a means of continuing what already is. It's also an emphasis on the fact that there should be more.

Because God is, and is infinite, the role that reproducing is to Being, is essential in Himself as a triune being. Reproduction, then, is the active belief that the infinite aspect of God is good. He is worthy to continue to be. He is worthy to forever be pursued and valued.

It appears that in the basic layout of the Bible, the triune God is put on display in a large simple way.

The Old Testament is highlighting God the Father, while the other two persons play supporting roles. The Son and the Holy Spirit are certainly present, but they aren't center stage.

God the Father can be defined by law, rule, boundary, and holiness. He is what is mature, fixed, complete, strict, harsh, closed, systematic, holy, judge, detailed, tradition, foundation, and orderly.

Following the Old Testament, the Gospels (the books of Matthew, Mark, Luke, and John) highlight the second person of the Trinity, the Son.

Who is the Son? He is embodiment, subjecting Himself to the law, willfully bearing all weight of the curse, experiencing its repercussions, and transcending them. He's the mediator, the tension, the journey.

As He makes His way out from center stage, he introduces the one to follow, the third person of the Godhead, the Holy Spirit.

The Holy Spirit is defined by the infinitude aspect of reality. He's associated with what is boundless, limitless, open, and free.

With the Holy Spirit comes a theme of reproduction and a move beyond the borders: "To the ends of the earth and all nations."

There's a sense of explosion. Things move from a very confined condition into a more chaotic, outward, energized, expressive, dramatic occurrence. There's multiplication. There's a transition from confined to that which is open. To the place that hasn't been reached. It's new, different, fresh, and unknown, the infinite.

It's no accident that the image given for the result of being connected to or rooted in the Holy Spirit is called fruit.

The analogy, "The fruit of the Spirit is . . ." (Galatians 5), is giving us insight into who the Spirit is, how He functions, and what His place is in reality.

Fruit is colorful. It's the resulting produce from the foundation and structured entity, the tree or plant. Fruit is also the initial product that will be used to initiate the beginning of the entity that produced it in the first place.

I mentioned the theme in the Bible of the barren womb. Sarai was barren, Rebekah was barren, Rachel was barren, Manoah's wife was Barren, Hannah was barren.

After hundreds of years of silence from God, we reach the New Testament. It begins with a woman named Elizabeth, married to Zechariah. She has been barren and now is in her old age. God, then breaks the silence, and speaks. He promises the couple a son.

Luke 1 tells us that Elizabeth will bear a son and his name will be John. "He will be filled with and empowered to act by the Holy Spirit while still in his mother's womb." (v. 15 amp)

Later in the same chapter, we are introduced to Mary. An angel shows up and promises her a son.

"Mary said to the angel, 'How will this be, since I am a virgin and have no intimacy with any man?' Then the angel replied to her, 'The Holy Spirit will come upon you, and the power of the Most High will overshadow you [like a cloud]; for that reason, the holy (pure, sinless)

Child shall be called the Son of God. And listen, even your relative Elizabeth has also conceived a son in her old age; and she who was called barren is now in her sixth month." (vv. 34–36 AMP)

The same description we see in Genesis 1:2 of the Spirit over the unformed deep, is what we see described in the passage above.

God the Father is not looking around trying to figure out how He's going to accomplish what He wants and then notices the Holy Spirit and asks Him if He wants to help out.

The Holy Spirit is uniquely defined and characterized differently from the other two persons of the Trinity. He is uniquely fit for the elements and design of the cosmos—history and reality—because those elements are designed and patterned after him.

He is about reproducing and multiplying, forever signaling and leading into the infinite.

13
Comfort and Restore

Because the Holy Spirit leads into new territory, there are dangers of exposure in the unknown. There is trial and error. He is also uniquely qualified to meet people in their failure, the valley and storm, to comfort and encourage them.

The song, "Gold and Silver" by Stavesacre demonstrates this. https://www.youtube.com/watch?v=KjS5Z-c1usI

Being free and out in the open also means being exposed and vulnerable.

The Spirit in Genesis 1:2 is hovering over the water, the deep, the unknown, and the potential. He's doing so with anticipation or expectation of something beyond what already is. It's a picture of a bird covering its nest of chicks. If this is right, then it is an image of new life; infancy with need for care and covering.

Because the beginning of something is undeveloped or not yet mature, it is vulnerable. There isn't any proficiency, development, maturity, structure or law yet.

It's the newborn, the new world, the revolution, the frontier, or the wild west.

It's man out from father and mother to cling to his wife. It's Adam and Eve out of the garden, Noah out of the ark, Abram out from his father's home, Joseph dumped by his brothers into the pit, Israel out from Egypt, Israel in exile, Jesus out from the tomb, the disciples out from the upper room, God's message out from Jerusalem to the ends of the earth, God's covenant out from the Jew to every tongue tribe and nation.

Going right along with the element of freedom and openness, is the need for covering. Every time you step out, or begin something new, it's a risk.

If it's voluntary, it can be an exciting moment or season. If it is forced or things don't go according to plan there is great need for nurture, shelter, and warmth.

Oftentimes we are left out, pushed out, kicked out, or fall out. Being forced out of the walled city, the paradisal garden, leaves us exposed with the need for comfort, attention, healing and restoration.

Oftentimes it can be the trial and error in a new space that makes us discouraged or depressed.

It's the Holy Spirit, the hovering dove, that covers the chicks because they are undeveloped and vulnerable. They are the future, the ones that move forward. The open infinite is real and good, worthy of stepping into. But it requires special care.

Once Jesus embodies the law, dies, resurrects, and walks out of the old, traditional, rules loaded covenant into the new era, He leaves. But He sends the Comforter.

When you walk away, shed something, or change, you enter new territory. There is risk of exposure to friction, pain, and suffering. But the Holy Spirit is present in the dark, the confusion, and in the chaos.

These are just the basic conceptual themes noted in the Scriptures narrative related to the Holy Spirit and the Trinity. If the Scriptures explanation is the true description of all things, and God used Himself as the blueprint to create, then where do these themes show up in the universe?

Let's do some comparative analysis.

14
Art and Dreams

Art "Music begins where the possibilities of language end."—Jean Sibelius

God is infinite.

Artists are the first ones to press into and articulate the unknown. Because it is the unknown, the artists are gifted to represent it. This means the representation is no longer completely unknown, yet neither is it fully articulated and understood. The representation sits between the known and unknown and therefore is dream-like and abstract. This is what art is, the role art and artists play.

God is.

God is there. He is defined, distinct and specified.

He has a particular nature. It has parameters. There is a border between God and non-God, being and non-being.

Definition and distinction find their origin in the reality of being. If there is no being, no thing, there is no reality of definition or borders. That God is, means that definition and distinction is necessarily.

These find their origin in the nature of God being something rather than nothing, something in particular rather than everything.

The lines of definition allow for the ability to see, know, understand and relate.

Knowledge, understanding, and relation find their origin in the reality that God is.

Definition, parameter, border, knowledge, understanding, and relationship are a basis for security, comfort, functionality, and home.

However, the claim of knowledge and truth can lead to dogma, legalism, arrogance, self-righteousness, isolation, and echo chambers.

This then, results in things withering, decaying, deteriorating; growing stale, becoming sterile, turning into stone and dust.

Truth

Truth has the characteristics of definition and precision, of being absolute, matter of fact, solid, strong, foundational, known, or understood. But the truth itself is open. It has the ability to update.

Truth in the Christian explanation ends up defined as a human living being. God, the law in flesh. It is not a closed domain, merely a stone lifeless singularity.

God is infinite.

At the highest and deepest level of analysis, there is an eternal need and priority to move forward, to continue. There is always more.

The infinite, by definition, is boundless. There are no borders or parameters. There is a lack of definition. The infinite is open and free. Infinitude pulls the dogmatic out, rejuvenates the wasteland, animates the dust, revitalizes the old, stimulates the stagnate, and resurrects the lifeless.

It's too easy to get stuck and become a slave, tyrannized by the limitation of what has been or what is. But now that we see that what is, is not only strictly defined but also infinite, we can dream, create, jump out and make things new.

We can trust that the same God who is good in particular distinction, law and definition, is good in mystery. He is unreachable, unsearchable, invisible, incomprehensible, uncontainable, far above what we can think or imagine. He is always beckoning, calling us out toward Him in the infinite.

This is what art does. This is what art is. This is where art resides. It mediates between the safe known and the open unknown. It's on the frontier, always exploring the vast wilderness. it allures, coaxes and dreams, indicating to us that there is an infinite beauty and good yet to be seen, had, and experienced.

"And without faith it is impossible to please God."—Hebrews 11:6 (niv)

Artists are the ones that beckon and inspire us to step out.

Art is experimental. It's a risk by nature. It courageously ventures out into uncharted territory, signaling back to us what it sees.

> When a city is decaying, in various places, usually it has to be decaying in a somewhat interesting way. The artists are the first people to pick up on the possibilities of what that decayed landscape now presents, and the possibilities are usually two-fold. One is, well it's cheap, and that's good for artists because of course they never have any money. But the other reason is that there's a place that could be beautiful again if someone just paid enough attention to it, and the artists are very good at picking up on places that are cool but a little on the unsafe side let's say . . . and that's sort of where artists live, because they have a niche. They have a biological niche, and their biological niche is, interesting and unsafe. And then the artists go in there and they civilize it and now the other people can move in, and that's what artists do.—Art Gallery "Tadeusz Biernot: 'Layers' Introduced by Jordan Peterson at Articsok Gallery." YouTube Video, 11:54, October 11, 2013. https://youtu.be/GR-lwWS9mTo?si=k23J_o6AtVO7vhaJ

In the scriptural story, musicians and artists always lead the people. They were first. They went out ahead.

"Now the Lord said to Moses, 'See, I have called by name Bezalel, son of Uri, the son of Hur, of the tribe of Judah. I have filled him with the Spirit of God in wisdom and skill, in understanding and intelligence, in knowledge, and in all kinds of craftsmanship, to make artistic designs for work in gold, in silver, and in bronze, and in the cutting of stones for settings, and in the carving of wood, to work in all kinds of craftsmanship.'"—Exodus 31:1–5 (amp)

"In the same way, the Spirit [comes to us and] helps us in our weakness. We do not know what prayer to offer or how to offer it as we should, but the Spirit Himself [knows our need and at the right time] intercedes on our behalf with sighs and groanings too deep for words."

—Romans 8:26 (amp)

"And do not get drunk with wine, which leads to reckless living, but be filled by the Spirit: speaking to one another in psalms, hymns, and spiritual songs, singing and making music with your heart to the Lord"
—Ephesians 5:18 (csb)

"And they were all filled [that is, diffused throughout their being] with the Holy Spirit and began to speak with other tongues (different languages), as the Spirit was giving them the ability to speak out [clearly and appropriately]." —Acts 2:4 (amp)

This is a description of the ability to operate outside of natural bounds in speech and language.

Knowledge, order, structure, home, and safety can crumble. The snakes inside can corrupt and cloud. They turn paradise into hell, throw home into chaos, transform security into threat.

We are constantly falling and being pushed out of the known and secure. There's abrupt change. Tragedy strikes. We lose a job, become ill, twin towers fall, marriage ends in divorce. We're victimized, the opposing political party wins the election, a loved one dies, a tornado devastates a town, and so on.

The artist is there to comfort and to encourage. Art has the ability to resonate with the human where explanation is lacking and insufficient. Reason doesn't reach to the depth of hurt, confusion, and darkness that we so often find ourselves in.

Art sympathizes. It empathizes. It's not only able to reach and be present with us in the unknown but is able to indicate that there is a better tomorrow and inspire towards it. "This present condition isn't the end. You can make it through," and the art will be with you to help you as well as celebrate when you do.

That is precisely what the Holy Spirit does.

I was up late the other night, and I heard the birds outside begin to chirp. At that moment I realized that one of the first signs that morning is coming is the sound of the birds singing. The light is still a few hours away. It's very dark, perhaps the darkest part of the night, but the birds wake up and begin to sing.

I thought, what would be equivalent to life experiences that are dark and trying, that would play the role of the chirping bird indicating that morning is coming? It must be the musicians.

Musicians are the first to meet us in the dark of night. Before we can navigate all the way through, know what to do, or that we will make it, they sing. They comfort us, reminding us that the present darkness won't last.

It was the psalmist, the musician who stated, "Weeping may stay overnight, but there is joy in the morning."

—Psalm 30:5b (csb)

"Trouble Don't Last Always" by Timothy Wright expresses this truth. https://www.youtube.com/watch?v=

Si-5nGEGtzI

That's certainly how the Holy Spirit functions.

The song, "Blackbird" by the Beatles comes to mind. https://www.youtube.com/watch?v=7epRPz0LGPE

If you want to get a glimpse at the unique role and function of the Holy Spirit, listen to artists. Listen to charismatic Christian artists. The very fact that they are less traditional, more open, and emphasize the gifts, power, and work of the Holy Spirit is right in line and rooted in who and what the Holy Spirit is and how He functions.

The popular contemporary Christian song, "Oceans" by Hillsong United, comes to mind. https://www.youtube.com/watch?v=OP-00FwLdiU

Art mediates between the known and the unknown. Its lines are obscure and abstract. It appeals to our senses and the depths of our psyche, indicating that we have the infinite to contend with. Art is good, because God, supreme being itself, is infinite, waiting for us beyond the limits of our finitude.

It's a thing that worries me sometimes whenever you talk about creativity, because it can have this kind of feel that it's just nice. It's not! It's vital! It's the way we heal each other. Most people don't spend a lot of time thinking about poetry. Until their father dies, they go to a funeral, you lose a child, somebody breaks your heart, they don't love you anymore. And all of a sudden, you're desperate for making sense out of this life. And has anybody ever felt this bad before? How did they come out of this cloud? Or the inverse, something great. You meet somebody and your heart explodes. You love them so much you can't even see straight. And that's when art's not a luxury, it's actually sustenance. We need it.—TED, "Give yourself permission to be creative | Ethan Hawke | TED", YouTube Video, 9:16, August 11, 2020. https://youtu.be/WRS9Gek4V5Q?si=slpIJH3HdlWkCBlV

Art is about God by nature. its intricately and forever tied to that which is eternal, right, good and beautiful, and in Francis Schaeffer's words, the one who is personal infinite.

Artists . . . we love you! We need you!

You are our lifeline. You're our comfort, our color, our vision, our voice, our expression, our feeling, and our inspiration!

Thank you!!

"Normality is a paved road: it's comfortable to walk but no flowers grow."—Vincent Van Gogh

Dreams

I used to have nightmares when I was little. Oftentimes the images of terror weren't so distinguished between when I was asleep or when I was awake.

Those experiences of horror were quite weird. I hadn't spent time watching the news. I hadn't seen horror movies. I didn't know any bad people, or evil experiences. I knew nothing of the horrors of history, or crime plaguing our communities.

Yet, there was something about the dark and the unknown that the deep psyche, intuition, and spirit were getting right when reaching out, sensing, and feeling around.

What in the world are dreams, and why are they apart of God's economy?

There is a theme of dreams throughout the Bible's storyline. Let me repeat that. There is a theme through the Bible exposition, of dreams. For my theologian friends, we would say there is a theology of dreams.

Do you remember Joseph? He is one of the leading characters in the Bible. He was a dreamer. What role did dreams play in his story?

Joseph, in part, functions as a precursor to the coming Messiah. Bible scholars have covered and demonstrated this quite well.

Is Joseph also a type of Holy Spirit?

Through the Bible narrative there are types of the Holy Spirit. There's oil, water, wind, fire, wine, all playing in part, the role of showing us the Holy Spirit. Elements patterned after and giving us insight into the nature and function of the third person of the Trinity.

Let's restate that the Holy Spirit is open, the initiator, explorer, a move from singularity to multiplicity.

Joseph owns a coat of many colors. He's a dreamer. He's the first one out from his family and into a foreign land. He has insight and wisdom in interpreting dreams. Even though he enters Egypt as a slave, he is able to navigate the foreign territory with great success. He ends up in the place where there is food in the middle of a famine.

Joseph, although not the line from which the Messiah comes, is the only one out of his brothers who in Genesis 41:38 is said to be filled with the Holy Spirit.

Revelations, the last book in the Bible, is like a hallucinogenic nightmare. It's imagistic, dramatic, weird, wild, theatrical, outlandish, and futuristic.

I'm afraid that the Christians who are skeptical of God speaking through dreams anymore are more out of a fundamental lack of understanding of what dreams are, their place and function to begin with.

Dreams communicate by nature. They explore by design. They are open, dramatic, charismatic, and implicit, rather than well defined, specific, and explicit.

Like art, they seem to mediate between the known and the unknown.

Like the Holy Spirit, they indicate for us that we don't have or know everything. The infinite has to be contended with. They are a siren, alarming that where we are not safe, or something is coming. They are an indication that we need to move, or where we need to go.

Like how the Holy Spirit is given to every converted believer in Jesus as a guarantee about what the future holds for them, so were the dreams Joseph had and was interpreting, functioning as previews of what was to come in God's plan.

Dreams function like a preview of what's to come. We are all familiar with movie previews. They give us snapshots of the full story. They give us glimpses of the genre, style, type of characters in the movie. But you do not get the details, the full expression until you see the movie.

The introductions to the James Bond movies typically function like a dream preview to the movie. There is a song, the images are very artistic and abstract, giving us a sense of what may be included in the movie.

Dreams almost help baby step us into what is not understood or known. They indicate that something may need attention, perhaps something that we are afraid of.

It seems that the organization and function of the cosmos is congruent with the nature of God. It can be seen in virtually every aspect and at every level of analysis in life.

I'm no longer that young child plagued by bad dreams. I'm an adult now. However, I am keenly aware that nightmares are real. But when I ask God for help, He stands up in the middle of the very great deep and says, "Peace, be still."

15
Liberalism

The basic framework in American politics is broken into liberal and conservative. Those aren't just differing values; they are diametrically opposed.

Conservatism is about preserving the tradition, having strong borders, and maintaining certain morals. Their priority is inward and upward toward an ideal. It's about security and competence, being strong and goal oriented.

Liberalism is about being progressive, innovative, open, and free. There is an emphasis on caring for and bringing attention to the marginalized. Their value is directed out and downward to those at the bottom.

Why innovation and change?

Without transformation or progress, things will grow stale, wither and die.

The liberal aspect in a society is necessary if that society is going to roll with the times, and not get stuck.

It is also necessary if there is going to be an adequate voice for the voiceless, the hurting, and those who have failed or been left behind. There is an emphasis on minorities by the political Left. It's rooted in this value of looking out for those who aren't the majority or at the top.

I believe these values are fundamentally essential. They are good, and right in line with who God is, how He functions, and reveals Himself as the third person of the Trinity.

One of the reasons why there is so much hostile division between political parties in recent years is because there is a lack of understanding, on both sides, of the true values of each party. Not that they are different only, but to state it a second time, diametrically opposed.

Ben Shapiro, a conservative political commentator and media host, has a line directed at the left: "Facts don't care about your feelings." That's rooted in the value of conservatism, the mind, orderliness, and accuracy. It is a true statement.

The liberal opposing statement would be, "Feelings care about more than just the known facts."

There is always more to be considered than just what is known, or just the pure factual information. Liberals remind the conservatives and the rest of us, that there is always more.

16
Emotions

The Human is a complex entity. There are many layers, levels, and elements that come together to form what a human being is. One of them is the inner being. The inner life has been described as being composed of the mind, the will, and the emotions.

The mind is the orderly, calculated, conservative aspect. The will is the mechanism that selects. It's the part that takes all info and directs it out into action.

The emotions can be described as being a first indicator. Emotions are not locked in tight. They are open, feeling and sensing. They are dynamic, explosive, expressive and perhaps, exploratory.

There is fact, faith and feeling. Fact is tied to our mind. Faith is tied to our will. Feeling is tied to our emotion. Emotions are liberal. They are out sensing what could be. They help navigate before we have all of the information. They function like an internal navigation system.

The role that emotions play for the inner life of the human is central for health and balance, all because they are unique and function differently than the mind. They serve, benefit, and inform the mind allowing for the will to operate with max input.

Emotions are not supposed to function like a calculating mind; organized, in order, and confined.

They are more chaotic, reactionary, intuitive, dramatic, fast, explosive. Emotions bring the moment to life, coloring it in, awakening the senses to the reality of the present, as well as indicating that there is infinitude beyond us.

Emotions help us to face reality when we are thrown out of order and into chaos. Our emotions are the first to encounter loss and change. Before we can grasp or understand what has happened, our emotions are helping us face reality.

"In that very hour He was overjoyed and rejoiced greatly in the Holy Spirit, and He said, 'I praise you . . .'" Luke 10:21 (amp). This is a reference of emotional expression.

"I will pour out on the house of David and on the people of Jerusalem, the Spirit of grace (unmerited favor) and supplication. And they will look at Me whom they have pierced; and they will mourn for Him as one mourns for an only son, and they will weep bitterly over Him as one who weeps bitterly over a firstborn." Zechariah 12:10 (amp). This is emotional expression, mourning and crying.

There is a reason why the book of Lamentations in the Bible story line is there. It's because it is in response to God's people being exiled, taken out of their home, and thrown into the unknown.

Grief seems to be a description of the myriad of emotions that someone experiences when they encounter loss or disorder, being thrown into chaos, out and away from the confines of home.

If the fundamental reality of God is that He is triune, then we could hope to see that reflected in our makeup. Emotions appear to sit in the triad inner make-up of the human as a pattern coming from the role of the Holy Spirit.

17
Female

What is a woman?

That is the question Matt Walsh asks in his film produced by the Daily Wire. It's a question fundamental to humanity, especially in a climate that is as turbulent as we are encountering currently.

Both men and women are equally human, designed and crafted after God Himself.

I think it's vital to state before continuing that there appears to be as much commonality between the two sexes than difference.

That being said, men and women are different. The fact that this has become a contentious statement is a testament to the times we are in.

> Boys talk about things and activities. A man's sense of self is defined through his ability to achieve results, through success and accomplishment. In general, men are more interested in objects and things rather than people and feelings. Women value love, communication, beauty and relationships. Men are more logical, analytical, rational. Women are more intuitive, holistic, creative, integrative. Women are in touch with a much wider range of feelings than men, and the intensity of those feelings is usually much greater for women than men.—© 2023 Relationship Institute, "Differences Between Men and Women." https://relationship-institute.com/differences-between-men-and-women

What makes a woman unique?

> So, I would say, when is reflexive empathy useful? That's easy. You're a mother, your child is under six months old, reflexive empathy is the right reaction. And I think that's why it's such a powerful motivating force as well. A child under six months old is always right. The child is in distress, always right. You're wrong, the child's right. No matter why the child is distressed, it's your problem and you should do something about it and

it's not the infant's fault. Ok, now we have a very lengthy dependency period as human beings . . . and because of that intense dependency, that empathic circuitry has to be very, very powerful.—DoctorOz, "Dr. Oz | Jordan Peterson: The Exclusive Uncut Interview | Full Episode" YouTube Video, 5:59:14, September 20, 2020, https://youtu.be/daVjWUCIbAc

The fact that this makeup and fundamental nature of the female is and has been criticized and looked down upon in our society for the last several decades by many, including feminism ironically, is a demonstration of ignorance. There is a lack of sophistication in understanding.

The virtue and value of having children and the complexity in their needs in development from conception through infancy is vital and fundamental to what it means to be human. That one of the sexes be uniquely crafted for a particular, significant segment and aspect of that development is not only simple to understand, but genius in its design and worthy of admiration.

It could not be more ironic that one of feminism's aims in the progression of women in recent years was to make them less feminine and more masculine.

If you don't know what a woman is and how she is unique in the first place, the chances that your priority to elevate and push her forward, are slim to none.

In the description of the resurrection story of Jesus, in Luke, it states,

> The women who had come with [Jesus] from Galilee followed closely and saw the tomb and how His body was laid. Then they went back and made ready spices and ointments (perfumes). On the Sabbath day they rested in accordance with the commandment. But on the first day of the week, at early dawn, [the women] went to the tomb, taking the spices, which they had made ready. And they found the stone rolled back from the tomb, but when they went inside, they did not find the body of the Lord Jesus.—Luke 23:55–24:3 (ampc)

Yes, it was a patriarchal society, in which the testimony of women in a court of law was not regarded as equal to a man. Yes, the fact that it was women who were the first to testify about Jesus is a testament to the validity of this record as well as a demonstration of God's elevation and equal view of women.

But, I believe, even more fundamental was that the women were the first to witness the empty tomb and the resurrection precisely because they were embodying what woman is.

The men were in hiding, cooped up, accepting reality as they most fundamentally saw it. And yet, it was the women who gathered the perfumes and ventured out, in the midst of the threat, at dawn, the breaking of the new day, to care for the body of Jesus. And because they did, they were the first to encounter the single greatest event in human history. Yes! Woman! Yes! Femininity! Yes!!

What is a woman?

"Venus" by Sleeping at Last begins to give us a sense. https://www.youtube.com/watch?v=2YbdBQpiaA4

A woman is the personification of beauty. She is wonder and glory in the flesh. Woman is the embodiment of mystery, maturity, romance, and compassion. She is the incarnate domain of beginning, emergence, dawn, genesis, and birth. Try downplaying that. You're a fool to try.

18
Conclusion

I was at the beach in the Caribbean, swimming in the ocean with a friend. We got into a brief conversation about risk taking; have I ever been parasailing or surfing? Would I ever go skydiving? I was stating my hesitancies, while she was expressing excitement at the thought of doing some of those activities. It was one of the most profound conversations I have ever had.

I was swimming in the vast ocean off an island, which was exhilarating. I was with a friend who was far more open to experience than I, and we were talking about taking risks and pushing our experiential limits.

The reason why activities such as swimming, surfing, and boating, are so fun and meaningful is because they are out, away from solid ground. They play with, push into, and contend with the infinite. That place between the known and unknown resonates deeply with the human being as being the right place and good place.

This was what I needed to see, understand, and act out.

Liberals want things to be open, free, new, and progressive. They bring attention to the less fortunate.

Emotions don't follow rules. They are constantly changing. They are out in front and ahead of thought.

Charismatics are about dynamics, expression, and the heart. They emphasize the presence, the power, and the spiritual gifts of the Holy Spirit.

Females are intuitive, beautiful, and sensitive.

Entrepreneurs are innovators, taking a business outside the safe bounds of corporation and into new territory and financial risk, to expand the current field of knowledge and expertise.

What the Holy Spirit is to the one true triune God is . . .
what art is to society
what singing is to speech
what entrepreneurs are to cooperation
what advertisement is to companies
what sales is to business
what emotions are to inner life
what energy is to the body
what dreams are to the psyche
what women are to the human
what mother is to family
what poetry is to literature
what liberals are to politics
what embassies are to nations
what evangelism is to Christianity
The Holy Spirit is:
the pioneer
the anomaly
the first responder
the alarm
the awareness
the hospitality
the sales representative
the initiator
the spark
the climax
the icing on the cake
the celebration
the finale
the fruit
the indicator that there is more, that there is infinitude.

These, including art, dreams, liberalism, emotion, and the female are just a few elements that are significantly marked out in our living reality and experience that seem to rest heavily on the eternal pattern of the triune God.

The Holy Spirit is about being free and energized, experimenting and exploring, reproducing and multiplying, comforting and restoring.

Kanye West is open.

Lady Gaga is open.

Robin Williams, open.

Prince, open.

Jacob Collier is open.

So, there I stood, in the middle of my church, my family, my city, and my home. I was committed to pursue what was most sure, bordered, organized, and understood. The whole while working to ground it in who God was as sovereign, perfect, orderly, and absolute.

Yet, as much as I strove to live there, the more the landscape around me began to shift, crumble, and deteriorate.

I didn't know it at the time, but I was in the middle of being alienated from my church, my home. The confusion and frustration of being misunderstood and disregarded by what I held dearest, was hellish.

I was born in this church, biologically . . . spiritually. I grew up there. I gave my time, energy and creativity . . . My Christian life is all intertwined within that community. My theological and ecclesiological development is all wrapped up in that church.

The church's identity is laced and knit into my own life and identity. That church has my identity woven into its history and legacy.

When I read the New Testament and its emphasis on the local church as a priority for Christianity, it's not an abstract concept to me. It's my dominant lived experience.

I know now why people walk away from church, leave the faith, or give up on God. It's no mystery to me anymore. There's an element that the teaching and experience no longer resonates. You become disillusioned. The relevance fades in light of deep harsh realities. There is something true and right about being honest about it.

It hadn't quite happened yet, but I could feel it. The absolute distress, heartache, and ruin from being torn away from my own life, my church, was coming.

I had two dreams. The first was several years ago when I was working on staff for my church. Our church building had four floors. In my dream, I walked into the basement, where there is an auditorium. The ceiling in that room was open all the way up through the roof, and it was pouring rain, soaking everything inside.

The second dream, I had a week and a half before I received disheartening news. It marked the beginning of the end of my relationship with the church.

I was in a neighborhood with some houses, but it seemed to be in a wooded area as well with plenty of trees and space. I was with friends and family outside when a wolf came out from behind one of the houses and started to head directly towards me.

I ran, but it chased me down. As it got near, I ducked, and it went right past me. The same thing happened a few moments later, only it was two wolves. When it happened a third time there were three; none of which were able to get a grip on me, even though they were after me. Once the wolves were gone, A large grizzly bear popped up, and sure enough, it started to roar after me.

As I ran, it grew closer, and I knew I couldn't outrun it. Once it reached me it lunged as though to rip me to shreds. But it just ended up brushing past, missing me altogether.

Once the bear was gone, I began to run again. I noticed that everyone else was running too. There was a storm coming and everyone was rushing for cover.

The houses seemed to be gone, and the woods thickened. As I ran and searched for cover, I found myself next to my dad. The wind and rain picked up in intensity. We both, in the same instance, dove underneath a large piece of something like plywood that was lying close to the ground across a tree stump. It seemed to be the best option at the moment. As I lay there, covered from the storm, I wasn't sure if I was actually safe. I felt safe, but time would tell.

While I was in the middle of writing this chapter, a friend I have had limited contact with messaged me out of the blue and shared this with me.

> I'm writing to tell you I had a dream last night and feel compelled to share. Only you'll know if this resonates with you. So, I had a dream that you were flying but it was as if you were new to flying, as if until this moment flying was foreign to you. My husband and I were watching you in the sky flying, you were trying to practice at getting better at it. You were struggling but you weren't giving up. Whatever it is you're going through in this season of your life, I pray you follow what the Holy Spirit is telling you to do, even if it's foreign and seems scary or intimidating, he will never leave you or forsake you; He knows what's best for you. Be blessed, not stressed, brother.

I was in the car with a few friends, my cousin one of them. He's in the medical field and hands down one of the most caring people I know. He was playing an album by a popular music artist and encouraged me to get the album for myself. I took his advice, and that album became one of the soundtracks for me for the next few years.

It was the last song on that album that really struck a chord with me. It was very soothing. It brought an element of peace that seemed to be a growing need as the dark months rolled on.

As I sat at the piano that evening fumbling over the keys, almost like the varying levels of reality aligning and clicking into place, I began to find the right note progression in that pretty tune. At the same time, I realized it was the last song from that album and how much it meant to me in the middle of the chaos—the piano sang out, "O" by Coldplay https://www.youtube.com/watch?v=-gA3H3clEqk

THE FATHER: A SLAP SHOT
The Tortoise and the Hare

19
An Introduction

I hopped over the boards, sweat rolling down my brow. Time was ticking. My skates hit the surface. O.T., finals game. It was "Go" time.

It was Saturday evening, a few hours from the close of the busiest week of the year. I spent that week as a staff member for youth summer camp. I returned home early that morning, got a nap in, tossed some laundry in the wash, grabbed a bite, and headed out to the burbs for roller hockey playoffs.

I don't know how I was awake and able to muster up any movement beyond a walk, but there I was. We played and won the first game. Then we waited a few hours for the championship game where we made it to the end of regulation in a tie. As overtime got underway and I made my way in for another shift, I was running on fumes.

We had the puck and tried to make a play but turned it over. Now they had the puck, skated it over the blue line into our zone, and they had numbers. Three on one, skating toward our net and I was the only man back.

If there's anything that describes me, it's defensive.

I'm careful and protective. I see all the risks and the potential threats. I like to keep things organized and in their proper place. Give me order and routine and I'm a happy camper. I live for tradition. I thrive inside of structure. A system makes sense. It's understood. I relish the past, am reminiscent, and cling to the known.

Mixed in all of that is the drive of competition.

There has been growing popularity in the criticism of hierarchies. The problem with the critique is that it views hierarchy as such as an evil. It does this without properly recognizing how deep hierarchy is built into the cosmic design as well as differentiating between hierarchy as such, and precisely when and to the degree it becomes corrupt, like anything and everything else.

Selecting is organizing things in a hierarchy by nature. Preference is exactly that. Prioritizing or having goals, is a generic description of hierarchy.

Being selective when denouncing hierarchies not only demonstrates the ignorance of how fundamental hierarchy is, but also the absurdity that you have to make a hierarchy to criticize them. Your thoughts and belief are that total equality and egalitarianism is best and should make everyone else bow to it. How ironic.

You cannot get away from paradox. It's impossible.

What if there was complete equality between people at every level?

I always wondered what would happen in a football huddle before the play if the players were egalitarian. Why does the quarterback get to call the play? Why does the quarterback get to decide who to give the ball to? Why does the team listen to the coach? Why is there a coach? There shouldn't be a coach.

Think about the rank ordering that happens when flying commercially. Everything from which airline, how much baggage, where the baggage goes, where to sit, the order in which you board . . . etc. It's nothing but hierarchy from start to finish.

Generally, women's and men's sports leagues are separated.

It is insisted that everyone and every type of grouping of people, including men and women, should be equal, and where inequality is present it should be corrected.

There is just one problem. Difference is built in at the very base of reality. Difference is where the beauty, uniqueness, and relevance of all is located. So, the insistence to make all equal just destroys the relevance of any one group or individual.

All are equally human, held as image bearers of the highest entity. But all that a human is and does isn't equal to all things for all time in relation to all others. The dichotomy of being finite in relation to the infinite is present. You can only be and do a limited number of things to a limited degree for a limited amount of time that will most certainly be different from any other. Calling that evil is not just ignorance of the design and function of the nature of the human being and the cosmos but is counter the nature of God. It is evil itself.

If those decrying hierarchy get the nature of hierarchy wrong, then they will get the diagnosis as well as the prescription wrong. This de credits the compassionate which in turn is a problem for all of us since we rely on them to lead us in compassion. Above all, at the very best, it neglects the oppressed, and at worst, it oppresses and hurts the disenfranchised even more.

Where are things like rank ordering, prioritizing, hierarchy or value systems coming from, exactly?

Aim

The human being is engineered to aim.

We are selective. Our thoughts are singular. Our eyes point. In the face of the infinite, extreme limitation is built in.

Vision is hierarchal by nature.

To say it differently, vision is a demonstration of the value or necessity of hierarchy. That you look at something is a demonstration of a value system. You couldn't see otherwise. You can't perceive everything all at once. Vision is selective and has to be, in order to function.

Our context is infinite. From the size and scale of the universe, down to the molecular level of matter, the infinite number of things to perceive, consider or engage, poses an actual detrimental problem.

The human being is finite and limited. We are seemingly designed for a particular function. The chances of us coming in contact with the infinite and functioning at any level for any length of time without falling apart or being consumed, are close to zero.

Aiming is a human fundamental necessity.

Aiming, through vision and the function of the mind, is the operation of selecting and the ability to focus. This allows for the human to be able to ignore the infinite and select a specific. This in turn allows it to take action. If there is no particular aim, then no meaningful and productive action can be taken.

It can be said that what we see is determined by our bodies. The body has a very particular design and function. Because of that it has very particular drives. The human being, including the body, desires and needs particular things, and that seems to determine the vision.

If you are walking through a forest, for example, and come across a tree stump, what do you see? An obstacle, a story, a seat? It's not a chair, it's a tree stump. But the body, in line with vision, accurately identifies it as a place to sit and rest, and that is in part determined by the shape, design, function and desires in the human.

Not only is the vision, determined by the body, seeing a particular thing out of the infinite, but it is also seeing a particular in that moment out of all time or any time. This is determined by the makeup, function, desire and needs of the body in any particular moment.

Sport is built around and on aiming.

Aiming automatically sets up boundaries and laws. It organizes and simplifies, determining specific action. Aiming, and boundaries that are set up as a result, leads to and welcomes competition and opposition. This adds a significant layer of drive, pressure, and drama, shooting the competitor upward toward heights never reached before.

God, in the Old Testament set's the aim. "Be holy, as I am holy," "I am the Lord your God." Out of the aim, just like we mentioned above, comes the law, the standards to be lived by. The law is the standard that you align your life to. The law is necessarily in sync with the particular aim, allowing the subject to function and actually move toward the goal.

When God states, "Be holy, like I am holy," He is setting a goal, a standard. It's a challenge for His audience.

A goal demands laser focus, ruling out the infinite number of options for action.

There is purpose in structure and restriction, in being bounded and disciplined. Its quality. Its improvement.

It's not only what is at the top that matters, it's the fact that there is a top.

God isn't just communicating that He is at the top and we should recognize that. He's showing us that the reality of upward aim, an ideal, the flickering star in the night sky, is a fundamental element of reality itself. It is good because it is rooted in who and what God is.

God is the highest, always. Not just in Him being a particular God among other notions or ideas, but because that rooted in the concept of God is the reality of the highest itself.

The term "sin," used often in the Bible and in religion, is originally an ancient sporting term. The sport of archery, to be exact. It means to miss the target.

Being patterned after God and engineered to relate to him means, He is the human being's aim by nature. This means that definition, prioritization, organization, and structure are built into our reality, in all aspects, necessarily.

Alignment

We were engineered to aim. Focusing on a single point, a goal, brings everything into alignment. Aiming directs our actions.

A friend of mine shared a story about when he was taking riding lessons to get his motorcycle license. He described how his instructor informed him about something called "Target Fixation." Target fixation is when someone becomes so focused on a particular object, they unintentionally ride into it.

My friend describes having a close call with a light pole his first time on the motorcycle, even after being reminded of target fixation.

If aiming was not built into our nature then we would be consumed by the infinite number of things to be perceived, or maybe even more technically accurate, we wouldn't see at all. If we aim at the wrong thing, we can fall into a pit or get into a motorcycle accident.

Having an aim or a goal, simultaneously sets up parameters and boundaries. It draws lines between the infinite and a particular. Having an aim, a goal, a standard or even an unintentional fixation, produces confinement and directs our action.

There is no function, understanding, or even perceiving without definition, organization, or structure. More than that, there is no created being without distinction or differentiation. It seems to stem in part from the reality of having aim, and that God is uniquely and always positioned above to be aimed at.

I was reading through the Bible several years ago and working through the books of Leviticus, Numbers and Deuteronomy. I knew that while wading through the detailed orientation of those passages, I needed to be on the lookout for the purpose behind and emphasis placed on such specific orders.

Let's be honest, if you have ever attempted to read through Leviticus, Numbers, or Deuteronomy in the Old Testament, you know what it's like catching yourself daydreaming or getting lost in the details and long lists.

I can open that same particular Bible and see where I highlighted the passages that gave the reasons for those details and lists: "Be holy as I am holy . . . know that I am God and there is none beside me."

The Old Testament in the Bible is significantly marked and defined by orderliness, structure, strict defining lines, detail, analytics, record keeping, patriarchy, systems, restriction, law, tradition, borders.

These defining elements seem to be present and necessary because of their relationship to the concepts of aim, highest and holy.

You cannot have the highest or holy without structure, borders, parameters and law. Those two values or realities are joined together necessarily. Logically, they cannot exist apart from each other.

Law, or something in particular like the Ten Commandments, is present and functioning all for the purpose of setting God as the highest value.

Having an aim or goal brings alignment. Alignment means organization, structure, or uniformity. When considering a term like uniformity we can make the mistake of thinking it means total sameness.

When sports teams wear uniforms, they are demonstrating their individual commitment to the shared goal with the other team members. It's the common aim that aligns the individual members and their differing positions on the same team. Even while the individual members have different functions on the team, because they share the same end, they are able to work together and help each other move toward that shared end.

Sports and competition demonstrate and dramatize this reality well. Sport, with its particular aim, boundaries, rules, and oftentimes opposition, is meaningful because it encapsulates this fundamental element of our nature.

The basic elements of sports are rooted eternally in God as the aim, boundaries and rules that are determined by Him as the aim, and anything present that opposes Him.

This description of God being the highest and defined by law, shows up in areas like sociology with a concept of hierarchy. With hierarchy, there is authority. Authority is being in a high position or being over an established structure.

There is an idea in recent years that hierarchy is evil, wrong, and corrupt. That it's rooted in a particular culture or time period. But if you take a look at the nature of hierarchy, it's clear that it is so deeply rooted in the structure of the cosmos, that the narrow, simple-minded critiques from modern society aren't critical or sophisticated enough.

Authority

The term "author" is present in the term authority. There is a sovereign ruling that comes with being an author or creator. If you create or produce something, you rightly have a position of authority, or rule. You are in the unique position of determining reality, to whatever degree, for what you have produced.

So, the realities of highest aim, and the laws or boundaries being in sync with aim, are giving us the description of authority. The object of an aim determines the law, parameters, and particular actions by nature.

Because God is always the highest aim with boundaries present at the same time, and all that is produced is coming from Him, authority finds its origin in Him. So, when God creates, and patterns the created order after himself, those elements are present and good because they find their origin in who and what God is. This makes authority, as such, an eternal good.

Accountability

With the reality of authority comes accountability. What it means to be made in God's image is that the human is tied to God just in being human. Because we cannot escape from being human, what we do and how we live, actually matters. It matters because we came from something in particular.

If our humanity doesn't line up with our source, or reality of what we are patterned after, not only will we be out of sync with reality but will be misrepresenting the reality we are supposed to image. If that image is perfect, good, right, always, and forever, then it will be to our own demise that we miss the mark.

There's a tension. In part, what it means to be made in God's image is to be sovereign beings.

God has a will. A will is a selecting mechanism. He made us in His likeness. So, we have a will. We can actually choose what to do. However, we cannot choose to separate our humanity from it being all wrapped up in, tied to and about God without natural consequences.

So, you can decide to do and be anything you want. That element of sovereign choice itself is a mark of being made in God's image.

But the moment you choose to be, think, or do something that doesn't line up with what you are supposed to image, namely your creator, you deserve to be held accountable.

An aim and the parameters aligned with it, produce the elements of authority. Authority demands accountability, necessarily. This is good. This works. This describes how God is and why reality is set up the way it is.

Aiming is narrow but enlightening by nature. Alignment is restrictive but unifying by nature. Authority is demanding but rewarding by nature. Accountability is rigid but corrective by nature.

20
Father

God refers to Himself as Father. We have human fathers. So, God is like a human father. Are we missing anything?

We typically haven't said much more than that.

What is a father? What does it mean that one of the persons of the trinity is the Father?

When God designs, He is designing with a pattern that is directly tied to who and what He is. So, if you want to learn or know about Him, you can look at what He has designed. God choosing to refer to Himself in part as father, is not arbitrary. It is giving us a significant indication of what He wants us to know about who and what He is.

He isn't stumbling across humanity, taking notice of how the human functions in particular ways, like fatherhood, and He is kind of like a human father and so decides to identify as a father.

Instead, He is taking the most fundamental framework that defines Himself and then engineers the human and the cosmos after that. It's precisely because He creates in this way that makes what He creates good, beautiful, correct, and functional.

When looking at God the Father, we are not simply looking at one of many attributes of God. More uniquely and fundamentally, we are looking at one of the three persons in the Godhead.

What defines fatherhood?

First of all, a father, or fatherhood, is male or masculine. Father-ness is all wrapped up in sexuality and gender.

Second, it is tied to the mother. It's not just male. It's not just any age or in any relationship or relational status. It is a fully developed male, in a covenant relationship that has produced. The father, being male, is unique. Different from the female mother, and to other males in general.

The father is established, mature, seasoned, defined, organized, systematic, the past, equipped and able to provide structure for protection.

Fatherhood, in part, seems to be the culmination of what masculinity, maleness and husband is.

It's a structural entity, made out of stone. It's strong, dependable, immovable.

In order for there to be beneficial structure, there has to be precision and attention to detail. There has to be solidity and structural integrity.

For the last several decades, the idea that the human being in all of its intricacy and complexity, is primarily socially and culturally constructed has continued to be peddled. This essentially means that there is no final eternal grounding for what makes up the most fundamental elements of a human.

Things like sexuality and gender are just reflections formed out of a particular approach to life and not rooted in anything final and ultimate. Therefore, they can be reshaped and reformed in the name of progressivism or improvement.

This may be a problem.

If they are technically rooted in something that is eternally correct and good, then attempting to change them could quickly lead to regress, corruption, and destruction.

21
Ideal and Judge

At the very center of the concept of God is Him being the final, ultimate ideal. In fact, ideal as a concept or reality originates in what God is. He is the highest, and the proper place for Him is always above.

Carl Jung has noted that any time you have an ideal, it necessarily becomes a judge. You cannot have a goal without it simultaneously being an objective observer that calculates what matches with itself and what doesn't. The very originating concept of ideal and judge, and their relationship to one another, is coming from who and what God is as the always and forever highest.

"I said to the arrogant, 'Do not boast;' And to the wicked, 'Do not lift up the horn [of self-glorification]. Do not lift up your [defiant and aggressive] horn on high, do not speak with a stiff neck.' For not from the east, nor from the west, nor from the desert comes exaltation. But God is the Judge; He puts down one and lifts up another."—Psalm75:4–7 (amp)

The human was engineered in every part of his makeup to have an upward aim, and to bear the weight and burden of responsibility to strive upward toward the goal.

If we throw out, downplay or misunderstand this ideal/judge reality and how it is tied into the nature of God, then we will deny and rob Him of the glory He deserves. We will be out of sync with reality.

God, throughout the Old Testament, is stating that He is the one true God, as well as demanding that His people recognize and understand that. He is commanding that they should strive to align their beings with Him.

"Do not have other gods besides me."—Exodus 20:3 (csb)

"Be holy, for I am holy ."—Leviticus 11:44 (amp)

One way to say it is, there have never been more demanding, burdensome and restrictive statements than the ones God has uttered about who He is and how we should see and relate to Him.

Anytime you have an aim or ideal, it automatically prioritizes one thing in the face of all things. This draws lines. It creates distinction and order.

When you have a goal and take action to pursue it, you are aligning with and subjecting yourself to something above you; letting it dictate the rules and parameters of how you should be and act.

This seems to be exactly how God in the Old Testament views Himself in relation to humanity. God is the Highest and He sets up the parameters in and around the Human to position them and move them toward God as the ideal.

We mentioned the element of authority above. Let's look at it a bit more. With God being the eternal standard, and parameters, rules and law fixed in place as a result, this describes key elements of the nature of authority.

Authority finds its origins right here, where God is always the highest end. That singular aim sets up the boundaries from the infinite possibilities of being. So, who God is, what He says, and what He does about anything, at any time, is from a place of authority. We are always under it, subject to it, and benefited by it.

That means, in part, that authority itself, because it's a necessity in who and what God is, is good. Authority isn't some arbitrary made-up social construct that came about through our learning and dealings over time. Authority is tied to God's nature necessarily, because of his position, function, and relation to all things.

How could God seemingly be so arrogant and demanding?

I was on atheist Dan Barker's Facebook page. He had just released a book titled, *God the Most Unpleasant Character in All Fiction*. I commented on his page, in reference to his fundamental argument in the book about God being jealous and that that is a detrimental characteristic. I commented that it was a faulty argument. The reason being, that if God was in fact the sum of all good and therefore the greatest being, then Him desiring all others to recognize that and be in agreement with it would be technically right, and therefore good. His jealousy is not out of some insecurity.

God is the highest and best, and that comes with the demand to recognize that and live accordingly.

22
Strive and Produce

God as the standard, the eternal right aim, means that in the face of infinitude, reality gets narrowed all the way down to a singularity. Everything else has to be ruled out, given up, or disregarded.

There are an infinite number of things that can be conceived of or be vying for our attention, technically speaking.

The decision to aim is followed by the act to strive or sacrifice for that goal.

Striving means having an aim and then working and sacrificing to move toward that aim. It's the decision on a particular and the rejection of all the rest.

This again, is built into the most fundamental element of how we function and how we can be alive, conscious beings. When I choose one thing, I am deciding to hold it above something else.

This is built into our eyesight, our bodies, our will, our thoughts. We are beings who select, and act based on our selection.

There is deep meaning in both the attainment of a goal as well as striving toward it.

"It's not about the destination, it's about the journey."

If God was there but not infinite, then reaching him would be the end. Everything would stop. There would be nowhere else to go, nothing to pursue, no further purpose to live, since all originate and culminate in Him.

If God was infinite but not there or present, then we would be in a constant state of pursuit without any particular aim or attainment. We would fragment and disintegrate under the sea of innumerable directions, options, and desires to pursue. We would grow weary and disillusioned. We would give up on pursuit altogether since it leads nowhere.

God is both there and infinite. The cosmos and reality he constructed matches that.

Both a producer and consumer engage in selecting and sacrificing.

The producer aims as an ideal and strives and sacrifices to produce what he envisions. The consumer aims at the ideal product and sacrifices to select and own it.

Here are some synonyms for "strive": endeavor, go all out, compete, contend, drive, fight, jockey, labor, strain, toil, bear down, shoot for, take on, try hard, go after.

Pain, discomfort, refinement or pressure go hand in hand with sacrificing, striving and producing. The fact that human beings are willing to face such opposition and trial at any point in time deserves an explanation beyond mere cliché.

God in the Old Testament is organizing and structuring the conceptual and lived out framework of His people with this theme of a goal. This is the practice of giving up what is held as valuable to that which is the most valuable.

The benefit of those particular things that are of value should never supersede that which the concept of value is derived from, God himself. Otherwise, the value in the particulars will lose their value and benefit all together.

It's not arbitrary or archaic that God demands sacrifice as a central means of relating to Him.

This concept of sacrificing what is of value for the greatest value seems to be at the heart of the Christian narrative. It is developed, beginning in the Old Testament, as the central means of viewing and relating to God.

At the heart of sacrifice is the value of production. It's a paradoxical concept that in order to produce, something has to be given up.

Sacrifice is the lived-out belief that there is more time after this moment, and more of things to be had in the more time to come.

Sacrifice, in part, is the means to produce. The best and most should be elevated to the top, so that the maximum number of things or people benefit from that reality.

To pursue God, is to not just have a singular aim that is good for me now. It is the belief that God is always the best for me now, for me always, for every aspect of what I am always, and for all humans always.

Because God is, in the words of Francis Schaeffer, "personal infinite," He is real, one that can be aimed at, related to, and forever experienced and pursued.

God built sacrifice into the created order in a variety of ways.

One example is, we go to work, sacrificing time, energy, skill, knowledge, pleasure, in order to produce. We produce so we can have a future, and so that our family can have a future, and so that humanity can have a future.

We and humanity having a future is good because it both reflects the reality that we are acting out how God acts when He creates. Also, it demonstrates that we are of value as image bearers of God and glorify Him by valuing humanity along with all of His creation when we prioritize our existence.

To sacrifice and to produce in direct relation to God then, would be an ultimate act for human beings. This is because its recognizing and believing sacrifice and production, as such, originate in God first and foremost.

Price's Law and the Pareto Distribution

There has been an insistence in recent decades in society of the value and priority of equality of outcome. The concepts of rank ordering, scaling, grading, and crowning have been under serious critique.

In little league, everyone gets a trophy. We're all winners. We don't want to hurt anyone's feelings. Everyone is the same and produces the same. Inequality of outcome is an indication of the presence of evil or at least that something is broken and needs to be fixed.

Inequality means injustice, is the ideology.

> According to Price's law, half of all scientific contributions are made by the square root of the total number of scientific contributors: thus, if there are 100 scientists within a given discipline, just 10 of them will account for 50 percent of all publications. Price's law describes unequal distribution of productivity in most domains of creativity.—*Dictionary of Creativity: Terms, Concepts, Theories & Findings in Creativity Research*, "Price's Law", Compiled and edited by Eugene Gorny. Netslova.ru, 2007. https://creativity.netslova.ru/Price~s_law.html

The Pareto Distribution, named after the economist and sociologist Vilfredo Pareto, states that 80 percent of outcomes are due to 20 percent of causes.

You cannot have freedom of choice and equality of outcome.

> Here's a nasty little law, as your company grows, incompetence grows exponentially, competence grows linearly. . . . The thing you want to understand about that 1 percent issue that you hear about is, it applies in every single realm where there's difference in creative production; number of records produced, number of records sold, number of compositions written.

> Here's an example: five composers produce the music that occupies 50 percent of the classical repertoire. Bach, Beethoven, Brahms, Tchaikovsky, and Mozart. So here is something cool; you take all of the music those people wrote, 5 percent of the music all those people wrote occupies 50 percent of the music of their writing that's played. So not only do almost all of the composers never get a listen, but even among the composers who do get a listen almost none of their music ever gets played. That's another example of this price's law scaling.

> It applies to all sorts of things, like; the number of hockey goals scored is also distributed this way. Number of basketballs successfully put through

the hoop follows the same distribution. Size of cities follows the same distribution. It's a weird law. . . . it's not a consequence, necessarily, of structural inequality. It's built into the system at a deeper level than that.

People talk about, all the time, about how unfair it is that the 1 percent of the population has a vast amount of the money. And 1 percent of the 1 percent has most of that money. And 1 percent of the 1 percent of the 1 percent has most of that money. But it is an inevitable conclusion of iterated trading games, and we don't know how to fight it.—Jordan B Peterson Clips, "The Weird Thing About Price's Law | Jordan B Peterson" YouTube Video, 5:45, February 15, 2020. https://www.youtube.com/watch?v=8z3OZ7QuJE0&t=29s

You can't have choice and equality of outcome.

To choose, is to aim. To aim is to select something preferable. The harsh parameters that necessarily follow selecting or aiming, is a fundamental reality of existence.

God, as a defined particular and always above all, determines that reality be defined by aiming and selecting.

23
Function and Understanding

Aiming produces structure and boundaries. This means definition. Definition, or even HD (high definition) as we are accustomed to hearing, means clarity, understanding, and knowledge.

The more knowledge I have of any particular thing, the better I am able to relate to and/or use it.

When something has form, it is in formation, I can know it. I have information.

Definition and structure allow for there to be knowledge, understanding, and familiarity. I can reside and spend time in a particular, defined space and it moves from being foreign and new, to home and family.

The formation not only allows for me to relate to it initially, in comparison to all other things, but to continue to relate to it and grow in understanding. It allows for relationships to move from surface and basic, to deep and well developed. That is the opportunity to function and thrive at a level that is very productive, beneficial and healthy.

Whenever you try something for the first time, it is often the least functional. It's only when you subject yourself to the standard and the trial and error of a particular thing that you grow in ability, skill, and function. You gain competence.

In my life, this familiarity or competence experience included things such as riding a bike, playing the drums, playing hockey, moving to a new city, making new friends.

The longer you remain in a particular place, the more you become familiar with and understand all that is present there. It's in part, what makes a place home.

Then, the more you participate and operate in that particular domain, the more you grow and develop in your ability to function and thrive there.

Sports dramatizes this concept for us. There is always an aim. There are always strict rules and boundaries, and there is always time spent striving inside of those bounds. This produces high level performance.

Michael Jordan was not the GOAT when he began playing basketball. It was the single-minded commitment to the game that drove him to greatness.

The same is true for any field or realm of study or occupation.

The aim and boundaries provide the parameters that allow for growth, development in understanding and function.

The Old Testament is displaying for us the reality that God values his relationship with His chosen people. He wants them to know Him.

How does He accomplish this?

By placing Himself as their aim, giving them specific laws and boundaries that are in direct alignment with Him. Then, holding them accountable to those laws, so that there is actual time and extended space for them to interact, live, and work out inside of this domain.

As a few examples, He accomplishes this through the body of the law, the tabernacle, the borders of the promised land, the temple, His promises, and His words.

This helps them come face to face with God Himself. This is good!

There is no personal God without Him being the epitome of definition. This is the fundamental theme we see in the Scripture, and more specifically, in the Old Testament. It also appears to be tied to the reality of God being, in part, Father. He is a perfectly defined structure that can be recognized and related to apart from all other realities.

24

Structure and Protection

Any time you set an aim or a goal, you get a standard that judges. But you also get boundaries that help rule out all other things. It provides borders and structure.

Borders and structure provide protection.

Structure is order, organization, definition, or the known. It's the Garden of Eden, the walled city, the tabernacle/temple, the home. Structure, the strict defining elements that dictate what deserves to be in versus out, allows for safety.

The reality of the infinite includes that which can overwhelm, consume, and drown.

We are limited creatures and cannot be in relationship with all things at one time. Living in a place and a space that is defined and walled, protects us from all that we don't know, can't conceive of or contend with, and not equipped to face.

It's the place that we run into when the flood comes, when the monsters are chasing us, or when the chaotic elements of life try to overtake us.

> He who dwells in the shelter of the Most High, shall remain stable and fixed under the shadow of the Almighty [Whose power no foe can withstand]. I will say of the Lord, He is my Refuge and my Fortress, My God, on Him I lean and rely, and in Him I [confidently] trust! For [then] He will deliver you from the snare of the fowler and from the deadly pestilence. [Then] He will cover you with His pinions, and under His wings shall you trust and find refuge; His truth and His faithfulness are a shield and buckler. You shall not be afraid of the terror of the night, nor of the arrow (the evil plots and slanders of the wicked) that flies by day, nor of the pestilence that stalks in darkness, nor of the destruction and sudden death that that surprise and lay waste at noonday. A thousand may fall at your side and ten thousand at your right hand, but it shall not come

near you. Only a spectator shall you be [yourself inaccessible in the secret place of the Most High] as you witness the reward of the wicked. Because you have made the Lord your refuge, and the Most High your dwelling place.—Psalm 91:1–9 (ampc)

There is no strong structure, able to provide shelter in the storm that is constructed without immaculate architecture.

God provides protection in structure, in definition, in law, in accurate calculation, and in the concept and reality of being the Most High. Protection and safety, by nature, are in the elements of borders and definition. This helps us aim and organize around God as Most High.

Structure and protection originate in the very nature of God.

The Past

The Old Testament is always emphasizing the past. The act of remembering is a major theme. Remember what God did, remember what He said. Remember His promises.

The past plays an important role. There is an emphasis on remembering to help provide structure and focus. It's there to provide assurance, knowledge, and an accurate reference point.

Time itself and our relation to it, in part functions as a triad. The past is fixed, the future is unshaped and unknown. The present is the mediation between the two.

Foundation

The Old Testament, being rooted in the nature of the Father, means it is defined by order, accuracy, the known and law. It's fundamental.

Law by nature, is foundational. It's tedious, detailed, long, and boring.

When's the last time you were on your social media account and went to your Terms of Use Agreement and read that?

Law has to be detailed and thorough because it's foundational.

Foundations by design need to be precise. They have to be well engineered. There has to be structural integrity. Everything has to be accurately measured and in perfect order. This is because it has to bear a particular load and take into account what is being placed on it and what it is supporting or producing.

When you look at a house to buy, and check the foundation, you aren't looking for beauty or style. You're looking for cracks. Will it hold up what is built on it? It has to be set, immutable, unshakeable.

Law is first. You can't make the rules of the game after starting to play. Play what? Play how? The law, the rule determines the game and parameters of it.

This pattern of law being foundational, first, or a standard and boundary, is how we generally function. A driver's license, then you can drive. A marriage license and vows, then you can be married. First sign the lease agreement, then you can live in the apartment.

This pattern works and is good because it's rooted eternally or theologically. The standard, law, and the state, then the incarnation, embodiment, and fulfillment. Justification, then works. Legal, then living.

"Righteousness and justice are the foundation of Your throne; Lovingkindness and truth go before you."—Psalm 89:14 (amp)

"Clouds and total darkness surround him; Righteousness and justice are the foundation of his throne."—Psalm 97:2 (csb)

The framework of reality isn't arbitrary. It's patterned after the nature of God. We can and have messed it up, but it's still present.

If you want to learn about and know God, study the cosmos, and all its areas of composition.

If you want to learn about and know the cosmos, study God in the varying layered ways He's revealed Himself.

The long, tedious, detailed, oftentimes boring articulation of passages in Exodus, Leviticus, Numbers, and Deuteronomy is normal. This is because they contain law documents, and law functions in this way.

All of the documentation of law at the front end of the nation of Israel's life is normal because they are a new nation.

That pattern doesn't just tell us something about God and Israel, but about God and all things.

God is the Father; tenured, tested, established. He is the authority, tradition, structure, order, and hierarchy. We see this played out, first and eternally, in the trinity.

The Son is the person in the Godhead who is subject to the Father. The Father is the one sending the Son. Those concepts are in the titles "Father" and "Son."

It's not by accident that God in the Old Testament is associated with law and patriarchy, being harsh, strict, orderly, detail oriented, systematic, and setting high standards. It's the most fundamental and defining element of who and what God is.

If that's true, then that precise pattern would and should be expected to be found in what He has designed at the most fundamental level.

Let's do some comparative analysis.

25
The Brain

The brain has two hemispheres. There is the right-brain and left-brain hemispheres. Why are there two, and what defines them?

In his book, *The Master and His Emissary,* Iain McGilchrist explores the divided brain structure and its utility. He states,

> It might then be that the division of the human brain is also the result of the need to bring to bear two incompatible types of attention on the world at the same time, one narrow, focused, and directed by our needs, and the other broad, open, and directed towards whatever else is going on in the world apart from ourselves.
>
> —Iain McGilchrist, *The Master and His Emissary,* (New Haven and London, Yale University Press, 2009), 27.

The right hemisphere is engineered for anomaly. It is concerned with the unknown. It's designed for exploration. The Left Hemisphere is engineered for routine. It's orderly. It compartmentalizes. If you search on google images for right and left-brain hemisphere you can see examples of how the brain hemispheres are defined and different.

In 2008 Neuroanatomist Jill Bolte Taylor gave a 'Ted Talk' in Monterey California on her personal experience and study as a brain scientist.

In this talk, in front of a live audience, Jill described what her experience was when she had a stroke a few years earlier and lost function of her left-brain hemisphere. She goes into detail about her perception of herself while having the stroke. It was no longer a solid, separate, singularity, but felt and saw herself as an open, expansive

force that was merging with every other phenomenon around her.
https://youtu.be/UyyjU8fzEYU?si=w9Zc1k8fGCeXeU7N

The two hemispheres are not just separate and different, but diametrically opposed. They are concerned with and value opposite things. The argument is that they are not just arbitrary opposites but the bases for opposite and difference as such, what is known and what is unknown.

The brain, however, functions as a unity. This is made possible by the fact that the two hemispheres communicate with one another.

The brain with its two hemispheres works to unify and become one in order to relate and work together with the body which is made up of all of its varying parts and functions. When the brain is in sync with the body, the person is a single unit equipped to contend with the rest of the world separate from itself.

So, there is supposed to be a constant movement from separation to unity. From multiplicity to singularity. Typically, this is happening in layers at the same time. It is the eternal interplay between the known and unknown, between chaos and order. This is what I understand to be happening in Genesis 1:1–3 and Genesis 2:24.

There is a pattern that moves from in and up in singularity to down and out in multiplicity and then back to singularity again. It's the move from the moral high place in the Garden of Eden to the immoral low condition ending with the global flood. Following the flood, there is a move up to singularity with the tower of babel, then its demise with the multiplicity of language and the peoples spreading out.

This pattern continues through the Bible. It is present in and throughout the cosmos. In the human body it can be seen in the design and function of the brain.

26

Competition

I had to be about six years old when I attended my first Chicago Blackhawks game at the old Chicago Stadium. From the moment of the deafening roar during the national anthem, I was hooked. Since then, I have remained a diehard fan through all of the ups and the downs.

Back in the 90s there was a Blackhawks player, Eddie Olczyk. After retiring as an athlete, he became a professional hockey analyst and is currently on television as NBC.'s top color commentator for NHL games.

I have watched several games in which Eddie was broadcasting and noticed something somewhat strange.

Even though Eddie is noted as a lifelong Blackhawks fan and a recognized figure in the Blackhawks franchise, when commentating for games, he would be objective in his analysis. It felt like he was betraying his allegiance to the Blackhawks.

It could be understood, when broadcasting for games on national television. In those instances, the broadcasters had to assume the objective position. Eddie seemed to do it well. But to be objective even when covering a Blackhawks game? That didn't sit well with me.

Was that right or good? How could he do that?

Something significant was at play. Something that I had already somewhat realized about myself, even as a diehard Blackhawks fan growing up.

I enjoyed hockey. I enjoyed watching the NHL, even if the Blackhawks weren't playing. I was a hockey fan before I was a Blackhawks fan. I mean, before, in terms of priority, not in time.

The Blackhawks were something particular in relation to something common, namely all the teams in the NHL. The Blackhawks are nested inside of the league. No NHL, no Blackhawks.

In order to truly root for the Blackhawks and desire this particular team to succeed, I had to be sure that the benefit and success of what the particular was nested inside of remained.

Particularity relies on the health and well-being of the common. I couldn't just be vested in the particular. I had to be vested in the particular and the common at the same time because of their relationship to one another.

What we were witnessing Eddie doing when He was commentating, was demonstrating the correct priorities in relation to the sport and the team he loved.

So, what is sport and competition, and why do we find it meaningful?

Let's take a step back for a split second and just state as honestly as we can that sports are significant. No case has to be made for that. Just watch humans. For better or worse, whatever sports or competition is, it has human being's attention, to state it conservatively.

Sport is a big deal. It's extremely meaningful to us. But where does it fit?

A particular team, in my case, the Blackhawks are nested inside of what is common to all teams in the NHL. The NHL is a particular league nested inside of what is common of leagues of all sports. Sports are nested inside competition or games. Competition or games are characterized by structure and aim.

This leads us to something which is nested in what we would define as an eternal defined highest.

So, there are two concepts here.

First, the particular elements that define what we call competition and sport are patterned after what God is, namely the first person of the Trinity, the Father. Because the realities of aim and boundaries are fundamental elements of His Being.

Second, in order to maintain the correct priorities in all areas of life, you have to understand that all things are nested up a hierarchy that is final in God Himself. He is the particular in which all true commonalities are nested.

What is most commonly true, good, and right about all particulars, anytime and anywhere, is defined by what God is.

The concept of archetype can be understood in this way. An archetype is where particularity and commonalty meet. If you took what was common among a set of particulars and localized them, you would have an archetype.

For example, God is the Father, because when and where the particular elements that make up any father are brought together, they find their culmination and origination in God.

Jesus is The Truth, capital t's, because what is commonly true and where truth shows up at any time, or what is true about truth can be traced back to the final defining element of who and what Jesus is.

The concept of God is, in part, the idea of archetype. What makes the God of the Bible the true God among any other so-called gods is that what is commonly and particularly true finds its origin and culmination in Him. So, if you find a particular truth at any point, anywhere, at any time, and you follow it up the hierarchy of meaning and function, you will end up in the reality of the God defined in the Bible.

Competition is regulated by and made up of a goal with boundaries to strive toward that goal, with the presence of opposition.

The decision by athletes to compete within the rules of the game and not cheat, is them subjecting their immediate goal of winning the particular play or game to the greater goal of winning more games. Then, more games for a championship. Then, perhaps, a championship for multiple championships. Then to be invited to play or participate in other arenas of life.

If they cheat to get ahead in a particular play or to win a game, they risk forfeiting the goal of the greater priority, winning at the highest level across a longer period of time and across fields of life.

What it means to be a good sport, is the right priorities of what the higher and lesser goals are.

"It's not whether you win or lose, it's how you play the game."

This means, it's not whether you win or lose this particular game that matters most but how you keep the particular game subjected to the highest aim and goal of being able to play as well as win at all possible games for the longest period of time. And you can't win if you aren't invited or able to play.

Competition is cooperative by nature.

We see this acted out at the end of every NFL game when the players shake hands, have conversations, trade jerseys, and huddle in the middle of the field for prayer. Even after all of their trash talking and trying to dominate each other in that particular game.

At the conclusion of every NHL playoff series; after the hard hitting, fighting, blood, sweat and some tears, both teams line up at center ice and shake hands, congratulating and encouraging one another. This is a dramatization that the particular game and series and oftentimes fierce rivalry is subject to a greater value and goal.

That value and goal, if pushed to its end, is to always have the opportunity and value of aiming, striving, and competing, always.

That value is nested inside the reality that God is the highest, demands that we recognize that and strive to be like him always and forever.

Athletes dramatize for us in real time and space the highest value of disciplining and conditioning the mind and body toward a goal, and that resonates with human beings at the deepest level. We've seen the Michael Jordan Flu Game.

Have you watched the last three minutes in Kobe Bryant's final game in the NBA? Lakers down by 10, Kobe on the verge of getting 50 points, takes over the game, and the rest is history.

You can be sucked in and be a subjective observer, focusing on Kobe's performance, or you can be more objective and just observe everyone else around Kobe. Listen to the announcers, watch the players on both teams, the celebrities in the fans, Kobe's family, the entire present fan base. Something important is going on here. This is resonating, at a deep, deep level. https://youtu.be/Rx2inwUj_F0

These moments, with the anticipation, the tension, the exuberance, the chills; and let's not forget all of the chirping and trash talking! We all have our sport, our team, and favorite highlights.

If you want to see mastery, discipline and achievement, if you want to see grown men cry, dance, and hug, if you want to see greatness, watch athletes.

Some things are not meant to be articulated and explained. They're meant to be witnessed and experienced. Competition resonates.

Athletes—We. Love. You!! We Need You!! You demonstrate God to us. Do well and keep it up!

This deeply rooted reality inside of the human makeup and function finds its origination and definition in how God has revealed Himself. Sports are a microcosm of the nature of God.

It looks to me, in part, it is how he has revealed Himself as God the Father. the Aim, the Authority, the Standard, the Boundary, and the Goal forever.

27
Leadership

Leadership is the position at the top, to look up to and be focused on. Leadership provides the point of attention as an ideal and means of direction forward. It is positioned up, above and over.

It contains what is developed. It's an ideal selected from the rest.

Leadership moves out or forward. It isn't just a stagnant, stationary ideal. It's in motion, moving somewhere in particular.

Leadership begins with integrity. Its foundation has structural stability. Structural stability is provided in and through being well integrated, providing unity and strength.

Integrity is having good character. Having good character means being well put together, which means strength and capability for high function.

Being placed in a higher position, is the recognition and acknowledgment of the presence of competency. It's the proven ability and demonstration of strong character.

If leadership is possessing integrity and good character, then it is fit to move forward, out and away from what is known and understood and into the future and the unknown. It is able to face obstacles without falling apart.

Because it is positioned above and first, it bears responsibility and the brunt of judgment, along with the damaging contact from all that is encountered when moving forward.

Simply viewing the high position as a place of privilege, primarily, and not responsibility, earned through character building, is a grave mistake.

The concept and term *elder* was already fleeting and faint by the time I was growing up. But in the last ten years, it has disappeared altogether. I don't mean the term used in church settings, referring to pastors. I mean the general term referencing those older and wiser.

The onslaught by our growing secular society and perhaps the secular left, in particular, against the hierarchy, the high positioned, masculinity, has sought to tear down and dispense with the concepts and realities that make up what elder is.

I've watched the role and position of leadership get attacked, torn down, and ripped to shreds. Not only at a distance, but right in front of my eyes. The insistence is obviously a critique of particular leadership. But after watching, listening, and feeling, it seems to be an attack on leadership as such.

Because it's so prevalent, intense, and happening at such a rapid pace, I'm having a hard time believing that the root doesn't reach all the way down to the pit of hell.

Leadership, in order to function, has to be structurally sound, well put together and strong, before it can move forward.

If it doesn't have integrity or isn't trustworthy, it isn't reliable, dependable, and able to hold together in the face of judgment or the complexities and pitfalls that inhabit reality.

There is no leadership without being structurally sound. It is the foundational element. There is no leadership without being an ideal, positioned above.

28
Personality

Personality. We all have one.

When I was on staff at my church, we went through an in-depth personality study over the course of several months. We each took personality tests and discussed the varying personality types and how they relate to one another.

The particular test we used was called "Livstyle." It broke up the personalities into four categories which included the Hammer, the Measuring Tape, the Duct Tape, and the Swiss Army Knife.

The Hammer is the achiever who is determined in action and production.

The Measuring Tape is focused on analytics, details, and quality.

The Duct Tape is concerned with the well-being, warmth, and unity between people.

The Swiss Army Knife is all about the experience, the excitement, and the possibilities.

The Livstyle program describes the Hammer and the Measuring tape personalities as task oriented and describes the Swiss Army Knife and Duct Tape personalities as people oriented.

The Hammer and the Measuring Tape are closed. They are in and upward directed. They value structure, security, competence, and quality.

The Swiss Army Knife and the Duct Tape are open. They are out and downward directed. They value freedom, the momentary experience, and those needing care and personal attention.

What we see, built in as the fundamental structure of personality for the human, is that which matches the same open-close pattern.

In a Ted Talk from 2008, Jonathan Haidt, an American social Psychologist, and author of best-selling books, including *The Righteous Mind* and *The Coddling of the American Mind*, states,

> It really is a fact that liberals are much higher than conservatives on a major personality trait called openness to experience. People who are high on openness to experience just crave novelty, variety, diversity, new ideas, travel. People low on it, like things that are familiar, that are safe and dependable. If you knew about this trait, you could understand a lot of puzzles about human behavior.—Ted-Ed, "The moral roots of liberals and conservatives—Jonathan Haidt, YouTube Video, December 31, 2012, 18:39. https://youtu.be/8SOQduoLgRw

Personality is so central to who we are individually. It's fundamental to what we value and how we function. We bring our personality to absolutely everything we encounter, no matter how great or small.

We are all familiar with differences between introverts and extroverts as it relates to social engagement. There are those that are more outgoing and those that are more reserved. There are personality types that are inward processors and outward processors as it relates to how people process information. They either process quietly in their mind or verbally, out loud.

The fact that the fundamental differences that make up the personality framework are between being open and orderly is quite fascinating.

29
Conclusion

What the Father is to the triune God is . . .
    what sport is to a culture
what the mind is to inner life
what the skeleton is to the body
what the corporation or CEO is to business
what the foundation is to structure
what man is to human
what male is to sexuality
what fatherhood is to family
what the marriage license is to the marriage
what the conservative is to politics
Michael Jordan is a high achiever
Hillary Clinton is a high achiever
Oprah Winfrey is a high achiever
Michael Phelps is a high achiever
Serena Williams is a high achiever

The puck was crossing over the blue line into our zone, three on one. I was the only man back. Skating backwards in the defensive position, I had two skaters to my right, the skater with the puck to my left.

I moved slightly to my right toward the two players, giving the player with the puck some space. I was showing that my intention was to attempt to take away one of the potential pass options.

As the play flew toward our goal, I knew the time for someone to make a move was closing.

In one quick motion, I moved from right to left toward the puck carrier, hoping to catch him off guard. I knew this would leave the pass option open. He passed the puck across in the direction of his two teammates.

As I skated backwards, the puck glided across the surface, now passing just a couple of feet in front of me. In that split second, I stretched my right foot out, somehow kept my toes down. The puck caught the tip of my front wheel and shot out directly in front of me!

In one fluid motion, like an Olympic swimmer flipping under water after reaching the one end of the pool and kicking off to shoot back in the opposite direction, I was now flying with the puck out of our zone!

I had a jump on the other skaters and there was nothing that was going to keep me from skating as hard and as fast as I have ever skated before.

My teammates were already in the offensive zone waiting for anything, a pass most likely. With my head down, skating across center ice, I had one thought in mind: "make the most of it."

As I crossed over the blue line and into our offensive zone, I took a look at the position of my teammates.

I was between the left-wing circle and "center ice." I knew what the goaltender was thinking—he had a lot to defend against. A pass would be obvious. I had a high percentage with shots on goal.

As I flew closer, I was about twenty feet from the net. I looked up, took aim, and let it rip. Over the goal tender's right shoulder, just underneath the crossbar!

In a split second my back was against the glass behind the net, arms in the air, my teammates skating toward me!

The goal was one thing, but that three-on-one defensive play.

The tortoise and the hare. The tortoise wins the race, not because of speed, but because of his accurate calculations, steadfastness, consistency, attention to detail, the precision and simplicity in his action and aim.

30
The Father and the Holy Spirit

Joseph, in the Bible story, has a coat of many colors. He is a dreamer and an interpreter of dreams. Egypt is the set-in-stone tyrannical state that purchased Joseph and made him a slave.

Joseph remains faithful to God and uses his dream interpretations to rise to power in Egypt. Because of Joseph's rise to power, Egypt loosens up and becomes more like the benevolent father who provides and protects the surrounding nations, including Joseph's family.

That Joseph ends up in this role and position, the representative of the state, gives us an image of God the Father as the highest benevolent one. Joseph is a precursor to the Messiah, he's a type of Holy Spirit, and he is a type of God the Father.

Joseph ends up in a high position of authority. He becomes the state representative. Provision and protection come from him. He plays the role of benevolent father to his family, to all of Egypt and the surrounding nations.

Once Joseph is dead and gone, Egypt closes back up and becomes the stone tyrant once again. Egypt enslaved Israel before God raised up Moses, a master of water, to lead them out of slavery.

Os Guinness, contemporary Christian philosopher and author states, "Reinhold Niebuhr would say there are two bookends of history politically. On one extreme, authoritarianism. All order, no freedom. On the other extreme, anarchy. All freedom, no order. The second is unlivable, and almost inevitably leads to the first, authoritarianism.

Now the American experiment going back to Sanai is between those two. It's an ordered freedom. The Lord frees them, they are set free to be free. But it's within the covenant.—Regent College (Vancouver, BC, "The Magna Carta of Humanity: A Conversation with Os Guinness," March 11, 2022, 51:43. https://youtu.be/2MqZgX0Qfxk

Covenants: God and the Bachelor

Is slavery a good short to long-term solution? If not, why not?

Is freedom, individualism or self-identification a right short to long-term plan?

The Bachelor, a reality television series, recently completed its 27th season on ABC. It's a show in which an eligible bachelor dates multiple women over the course of several weeks in hopes of finding true love. Through a rose ceremony, he eliminates some women every week and by the end selects one to marry.

God uses marriage as an analogy, because it is analogous, throughout the Bible storyline to refer to his relationship with those from the human race He has chosen.

No matter how you get there, dating, courting, arranged, or a television series, Marriage is a covenant.

What's a Covenant?

A covenant is a legal and affectionate relationship. If that is true, what does it tell us about who God is?

God is lawful and affectionate. He's just and loving.

> First, God is a standard, holy, lawful, perfect, in order, just, the objective moral line between good and evil.
>
> Second, God is living. He feels, has desire, has emotion, is open, gracious, and personal.
>
> Third, God has a will, a selecting mechanism. He chooses one thing over another. God's will uses both His lawfulness and His affections to select.

We are made from this tri pattern; law, affection, and will. A covenant is this tri pattern, which God uses to relate to us. That's what makes a covenant good and correct.

Have we been separated from God? Have we lost the concepts of God that perhaps we used to have?

It is now the norm, in our godless society, to think that a couple can cohabitate. It is enough to simply express one's love for another with no need to make it legal.

"I don't need a piece of paper to love."

"Why does marriage have to be recognized by the state? My love and affection should be enough."

"Who said marriage can only be between a man and a woman?"

"You can't tell me who I can love. Love is love."

"I can be whatever I want to be. If I feel like a woman in a man's body then, I am a woman."

Affection, feeling, or desire cut away from a standard, definition, or law, leads to chaos or meaninglessness.

There's a flip side. I have had conversations with friends in Kazakhstan who grew up under the Soviet Union. I recently read the *Gulag Archipelago* by Alexander Solzhenitsyn, which is about the work camps in the Soviet Union.

Law enforcement would break into their home in the middle of the night if they were suspected of speaking negatively about the government. Then, if they were found guilty, in a corrupt hearing, they would be shipped off to a work camp for fifteen years or more, under the most horrific conditions.

Tyranny, authoritarianism, totalitarianism is a government which "knows what is best for everyone." It is committed to usher in the utopia, as long as you completely subject yourself, your family, and your community to it.

There are plenty of nations right now as modern-day examples, to add to list the horrors of the twentieth century.

Law, cut away from individual sovereignty, produces slavery.

Tyranny violates the will and affection, by compelling obedience through force. You become stuck, like being in solitary confinement.

Individualism or self-identification, cut off from a standard, violates righteousness and the will, by lowering it, making it equal with all other choices. As a result, there is no way for the desires or affections to truly know what is best, what is right or wrong. You become lost, like being on a raft in open seas.

If you want things perfect and done right, you create robots. If you want thoughtless affection and worship, you have pets.

A covenant accommodates the standard and the heart. Covenant holds the law and affection at the same time. God's ways and standards are high and strict. But He also condescends. He's personable, relatable, and gracious.

The Bachelor points to something good. Unfortunately, its execution is reflective of our lost, secular society.

God, the Rose of Sharon, when He calls out and selects a sinner, He has the authority to change their name, as well as the heart to love and be faithful to them forever.

The Father and the Holy Spirit

If you distilled every structural design, of every field, at every level, down to its lowest resolution, you would see the same pattern, the description of the

Trinity.

God replicated this pattern and layered it into His creation. It's something like matryoshkas, the Russian nesting dolls. Or if you have ever seen one of those images that is made up of many of the same image, in various forms or colors.

While each person of the Trinity is fully God, each does not exist without the other two existing. There is goodness for each person to exist, in part or perhaps primarily because of how each person is particularly defined and how they each relate to one another.

There is a relationship dynamic that is present between order and chaos. There would be a downside if one was disregarded or chopped out. Each element, because of their unique characteristics, helps pull, by their fundamental nature and definition, the other back and away from being a standalone.

A few years back, I had two close friends, who separately were emphasizing a theme to me with one word. They repeated each word for me over the course of a few years. The first friend's word was "slave." The second friend's word was "freedom."

The emphasis of being a slave was rooted in the theology of being subject to God. The emphasis of freedom was rooted in the theology that we are free in God, no longer bound.

Neither of them knew that the other was emphasizing each theme to me. I was well acquainted with each doctrine, but it hit me at some point that each was true and yet seemingly opposed to the other. Both rooted in the same place, the central message of Christianity.

Here is an excerpt from a sermon by theologian and apologist, the late Timothy Keller, who pastored in Manhattan, New York, for several decades. It's on the prodigal son, preached from Luke 15, on September 11, 2005.

He begins by stating, "Tonight, we're going to look at a text that's been crucial in my life and crucial in the life of Redeemer (the name of his church)." He states,

> There are two sons. One is very, very good. One is very, very bad, and they're both alienated from the father's heart. . . . What you have in front of us here, are the two basic ways that human beings try to make the world right, to put themselves right, and to connect to God. Moral Conformity and Self Discovery. Moral conformity people say, "I'm not going to do what I want to do, I'm going to comply, I'm going to submit, I'm going to be good, I'm going to work hard." Self-Discovery says, "I'm going to decide what is right for me, I'm going to decide what is right or wrong for me, I'm going to do what I want to do. I'm going to live as I want to live. I'm going to find my true self." . . . The elder brothers of the world divide the

world into two. They say the good people are in and the bad people, you, are out. And the Younger brothers do as well. The self-discovery people also divide the world in two. They say, "the open minded, progressive minded people are in, and the bigoted and judgmental people are out, you."—Gospel in Life, "The Prodigal Sons—Timothy Keller [Sermon]", YouTube Video, August 10, 2015, 38:45. https://youtu.be/lsTzXI7cJGA?si=-PXF7971Iv-qpq1A

The older brother plays out the role of orderliness, keeping in line with the law. The younger playing the role of being open, anything goes.

If Keller is right, then right and goodness is not regulated to conservatism, orderliness, purity, and achievement. The line of morality is not drawn between order and chaos. I thought it was.

This is precisely what I believed. It was the exact point where I was stuck and wrong.

On the flip side, right and goodness is not regulated to freedom and compassion. The line of morality is not drawn between order and chaos or purity and tolerance.

This is worth taking the next two weeks, two years, or twenty years, and contemplating.

Orderly people so desperately need people that are open. They are so rigid and locked in tradition. They get stuck in what has worked before. They become focused on producing more and making gods out of heroes of the past. They need open people to grab them and say, "You are too attached! there is so much more! Could you also take a moment and look at those around you that are in desperate need? Loosen up! Open your heart!"

Open people so desperately need people that are orderly. They are so chaotic and directionless. They are big dreamers, in la-la land, disconnected, all over the map, dramatic and bite off more than they can chew. They need orderly people to pull them down out of the clouds of fantasy land, and say, "You are lost! Here are the facts. We've tried that already and here is the list of ways that it went wrong. This is what we know. Here is what we have learned so far."

Inside of Christianity you find this order/chaos and mediating framework in and throughout its teaching and history.

First off, the entire Bible is laid out matching this pattern. The Old Testament as the law, the state, the patriarchy, holiness, God as the beginning, foundation, standard, and Judge.

The Gospels as the law embodied and fulfilled. It's God in flesh, the Mediator, the Son as Humble Sacrifice, Conqueror, Savior, and Lord.

The book of Acts and the rest of the New Testament as the explosion, out from tradition, the unconventional, from one nation to all nations.

Salvation is justification and law. Then sanctification, acting out the salvation. It's trial and error. Then glorification, the finale. The end product and celebration.

The fundamental difference between Calvanists and Arminians seems to be this same order-chaos framework. Calvinists are tight, closed, strict, heady, and academic. Arminians are open, free, and people oriented. They lead with their heart.

There is complementarianism—which says that there is a particular order and specified roles for men and women, husband and wife. There is difference and hierarchy.

Egalitarianism—Which emphasizes the equality between men and women, husbands and wives. It emphasizes sameness. There is no distinction in role and function.

There are fundamentalists and cessationists. Those who emphasize the authority of the Word of God and believe the gifts and miraculous works of the Holy Spirit ended with the apostles in the New Testament.

Then there are the charismatics who emphasize the presence, power, and work of the Holy Spirit and who believe the miraculous gifts are still present today.

There are the extremes that mark church history such as absolutism, we are the one and only true church. On the other side there is universalism, all are welcome, we are open and free.

There is legalism on one side, those who value law and drawing lines above all else. Then there is Christian liberty, those who emphasize to permit all things because God is all accommodating.

Growing up, I heard that Christianity wasn't about religion, but was about a relationship.

Why are there so many significant differences and divisions at different levels of analysis on this axis?

God is the God of truth, the ultimate Lord and judge. God is the God of Love, the ultimate sacrifice and one who welcomes the worst of us.

Jesus is Lord, the master, the final authority, the head who should be bowed down to. Jesus is Savior, the sacrificial Lamb who goes out, subjecting Himself to the terror of the darkest darkness and the evilest threats, to reach us and love us.

All of these, just as a sample from Christianity, match this order/open pattern.

The conservative, logically minded, need to hear and have it said to them, in a simple manner, that the liberal, the emotional, the charismatic, open and free way of life is a normal aspect of reality. It's calculated into the design. It's a part of the whole master plan. It's central to the fundamental element of life. It's okay. It's good. It needs to be celebrated, valued, and accepted.

The liberal, charismatic, free and open hearted, need to hear it expressed and articulated to them graciously and sincerely that the high achieving, conservative, orderly, productive, analytical, up tight, strict, logically minded is a normal aspect of life. It's okay. It's good. It's beautiful. It's a central role in the picture of reality. It's needed. It should be valued, appreciated, and celebrated.

Both are supposed to, and by their very differing positions, see the dangers and downsides of the other. Both, naturally, without even having to think or feel much about it, are in tune and sensitive to how the other can go wrong and be out of sync with reality and drag everything to hell.

But our criticisms will only grow in benefit as we learn to study, understand, appreciate and value the make-up, structure, and design of the other. They are different. The reality of difference finds its origin in these two.

The mind needs emotions. The liberal needs the conservative. The man needs the woman. The dreamer needs the achiever, and so on.

How do these two come together?

You don't just hold hands, sing "Kumbaya," and call it a day.

How do they coexist? How could they ever link and partner to face the reality of that which was, is, and is to come?

THE FOOL: A MUG SHOT
Why did the chicken cross the road?

31
An Introduction

Are there any human emotions you think are overrated, underrated?

I think contentment is overrated. I think the human being is designed to lean forward, and that's when it is at its healthiest condition. When it's leaning into a slight wind. When you take away that resistance, I think it unbalances the organism. That's why no one's ever written anything funny at a beach. There's just no resistance. There's not enough resistance. That's why New York is the best place for a comedian. Because it resists life. And comedy comes out of resistance. The further west you go, the less funny things get. LA is less funny than New York. Hawaii would be the worst place to be a comedian. And then if you went to Tahiti, I guarantee no one has said anything funny in Tahiti in a thousand years.—The Media Stash, "60 Minutes: Jerry Seinfeld", YouTube Video, August 11, 2021, 29:00. https://youtu.be/OMOeWXq2Sz8?si=aBiOHjQ_f9QJZZ1W

The thing about standup, it's a bit of brutality that you have to have.—Jerry Seinfeld, *Comedians in Cars Getting Coffee*. Sony Pictures Television, Embassy Row, Columbus 81 Productions Netflix, 2012, https://www.netflix.com/title/80171362

"Why So Serious?"—Nolan, Christopher director, *The Dark Knight*, USA: Warner Bros., Warner Bros. Pictures, FilmFlex, 2008. Film.

Comedians are truth tellers. They point to the failure and the pain. The jester in the king's court . . . What's he doing there?
For "whatever reason" he's allowed to say things that no one else is allowed to say in the presence of the king and not have his head chopped off and delivered on a platter. Comedy seems to be an element of speech that plays a particularly unique role.

What is that role and why is it unique?

32
Speaking Truth to Pain

My brother and I loved to spend time with our grandfather when we were kids. But there was something my grandfather noticed that he regularly stated when it came up.

Any time my grandfather mentioned something tragic in a story he was telling, or perhaps in something we were watching on tv, my brother and I would get tickled and laugh. I think my grandfather noticed something in us, that was common among all humans, when it came to what was funny, and essentially what comedy is.

There is something about failure and pain, when we observe it, makes us break out in laughter. There are thousands of video compilations on the internet, for example, that are of people failing or failing. They are often labeled, 'Fail' videos. Made for the primary purpose of comedy. This is weird.

Any time we attempt to move up a hierarchy or progress out and away from convention and tradition, failure is waiting. It's built into the journey. This makes reaching the destination that much more difficult.

Yet, along with the failure and pain that accompanies the attempts at progress, is pleasure.

There's a mechanism that states, "It's okay. This is normal. Failure is a part of the process. Don't be so serious that you become resentful or bitter or give up." It's an emotion and a response that's so deep and instantaneous that it's not followed by thought, but by laughter. It's just how we are engineered.

Here are a few excerpts from Jerry Seinfeld's hit show *Comedians in Cars Getting Coffee*, a show in which he spends time hanging out with other comedians.

This is the most senseless profession on earth. I was born with this eyeball that sees everything different. Tragedy strikes . . . I got news for you; we have the jokes that night. Now, we know that we can't bring this to the public yet, 'cause we'll get hammered. But in a room alone, it's just us, we have the jokes already ready.—Steve Harvey

Fear is funny, especially when it's not fake. We're so used to fake fear. Everyone always acts scared, pretends they're scared.—Jerry Seinfeld

That's something in comedians I admire, the ease and lightness with which some of them can address very intense topics.—Christoph Waltz

One point is important here is, all comedians are artists, to get to something good we have to go down the wrong path, that's comedy.—Jerry Seinfeld

—Jerry Seinfeld, *Comedians in Cars Getting Coffee*. Sony Pictures Television, Embassy Row, Columbus 81 Productions, Netflix, 2012, https://www.netflix.com/title/80171362

If you spend any time listening to stand-up comedians, some of their best and funniest material is coming from the elements of their life that were most difficult or controversial. Their ability to talk about, and by no means downplaying the dark side of it but in a paradoxical way bringing it to light, indicates that it's real, yet it's not the end. Its ok, it's a part of life, and there is a pathway beyond it.

It's as if the comedian plays the role of initiating healing. They bring out what is deep, what is ignored, what is feared, and they pull it all out and say, "this is real and should be given some attention". They do it in a way that everyone agrees with and is able to face because it's done in the most generous pleasurable way possible, even though it's something dark, painful, or difficult.

Sophie Scott has a Ted talk on YouTube, in which she discusses what her research has discovered on laughter and its different functions. She says one of the significant roles that laughing plays is its ability to unite and heal people. Laughter, they say, is the best medicine.

One of the things that makes comedy work, and especially in a context like stand up is, you are sitting in a room with several other people, if not hundreds, sometimes thousands. Most of whom you have little to no relation. Another human is standing in front of the crowd and somehow says something extremely specific that you have thought, said or did, that you are ashamed of, or thought was unique to you and that no one else really knows about.

The fact that the comedian knows that, catches you by complete surprise. Not only that, but it resonates with the entire audience. So those multiple layers hitting at one time in a single moment, just produces an explosion of simultaneous laughter.

It seems good for the individual and the collective, that we share far more in common with one another than we may like to admit or realize. It's the fact that we are all valuable, on a journey, and that failure, pain, and difficulty is a part of it.

Comedy, in part, seems to be the element of being which goes out and provides an immediate relief to the overwhelming aspects of life and the pain it produces. It's a reminder that it's not over. This moment of pain and suffering isn't the end. If anything is true, it's this ... there is always, always more. Infinitude is at the bottom of the bottom.

I asked my sister about some of what she learned while attending massage school.

> I learned that being ticklish was just another way of knowing someone was guarded. Sensitive areas on the body are usually the ones that are most untouched. For example, under the arms or around the stomach or side. Some people have unusual areas of the body that are ticklish or guarded. This is usually linked to memory, and if not memory, then the unknown.
>
> Being tickled, while likely producing laughter, is also producing fear. The fear of the person not stopping or getting hurt by the one tickling. As mentioned, memory can also trigger a knee-jerk reaction of "I need to protect myself."

Because the body is all connected, muscle, in a strange sense, has memory. This is called "muscle memory." This could be any particular physical activity like a dance we learned as a kid, or a song we learned on the piano in high school. We surprise ourselves by remembering certain things that we seem to have forgotten, but our brains are more powerful than we realize. Sometimes we drive to work, something we do every day, and when we arrive, we can't remember the actual drive and being aware of all the turns we had to make to get there.

This can be true in the negative sense as well. A physical injury in a car accident, physical abuse, a fall down the stairs, are all examples of this [muscle memory].—Angela Lyons

So, being ticklish is tied to being guarded. You're ticklish in the more sensitive areas or places where there were physical injuries from the past. That pattern seems to be the case in relation to our emotions and psyche as well.

Why do you laugh at what you laugh at?

33
Speaking Truth to Power

I have a friend who was a part of an improv program a few years back, here in Chicago. I remember asking him a question about how comedy is positioned in life and why it works. In a part of his response, he said that comedy is always directed upward.

Comedy criticizes up the hierarchy. Almost to say, "I see you up there. Yeah, you may be in a better position, have accomplished more than the rest of us, but let's take a moment and look at where you are a complete lunatic."

I'll never forget sitting with two friends, watching one of Michael Jackson's recorded concerts. Both of these friends had the highest admiration for M. J. as an artist and couldn't praise him enough.

But, without skipping a beat, they were on to the vast array of ways he was completely over the top, quirky, and weird. They had a field day making fun of him, all the while still holding and maintaining the highest admiration and respect and praise for him. That really stuck with me.

On an episode of *Comedians in Cars Getting Coffee* with guest Joel Hodgson, Jerry Seinfeld explains, "The other thing that's fascinating, that I've found of comedians of all kinds . . . the corporate environment. The idea of bosses and employees is just hilarious to us. Why is that so funny? . . . It's such a typically human attempt to organize what is un organizable . . . life. We just see the hopelessness of trying to organize human endeavor into a building."—Jerry Seinfeld (Ibid)

The jester in the king's court, was allowed to speak truthfully to power, because of the understanding that no matter how well things are structured, how high the attainment or great the accomplishment, there is always room for improvement. The first step in improvement and progress would be to address the shortcomings and weaknesses.

The fool is the embodiment of failure, goofy, and unkempt. The fool demonstrates to those above and to the rest of us, 'this is a normal aspect of Being. This is what you want to learn from and overcome.'

Another excerpt from the same show, "In stand up, you kind of want a mongrel, creepiness, troll-like, out from under a bridge, individual..." —Jerry Seinfeld (Ibid)

If the king, the state, can't tolerate the comedian, the jester, then the state, the kingdom, isn't free. One way to determine if you are governed by tyranny or by a good king is the by the freedom of the comedian. The comedian is a characterization of the logos. The health of a state is determined in part by the primacy of the logos in that state.

The comedian seems to be uniquely positioned among everybody to point out honestly where everyone doesn't have it altogether. Nobody is safe around the comedian, and that's the point.

34

The Fool to Master: Part One

"Alrighty then!"
"Do not go in there! Whew!"
"Yes, Satan?"
"Lew-who, Za-her!"—Shadyac, Tom director. *Ace Ventura: Pet Detective*. USA: Warner Bros. 1994, Film.

I was out in the middle of South Dakota, playing on a playground in a state park in the mid 90s. It was my sister and me and there was this other kid there that we didn't know. He was repeating these lines. They were really funny. I finally stopped him and asked, "What are you saying?" He replied, "The new Ace Ventura Movie. Jim Carey."

I didn't know Ace Ventura or Jim Carey. But I certainly became familiar with those movie quotes.

Comedies put failure on display for us, and in a way that we can laugh at and identify with. The characters are fools, but through their failures in the story, they typically find redemption.

"There's an idea that Jung developed about the trickster and the jester and the comedian. The trickster is the precursor to the savior . . . Why? Cause you're a fool when you start something new. So, if you're not willing to be a fool then you'll never start anything new, and if you never start anything new then you won't develop. So, the willingness to be a fool is the precursor to transformation, and that's the same as humility."—Jordan B Peterson, "Lecture: biblical Series IX: The Call to Abraham", YouTube Video, August 1, 2017, 2:35:13. https://youtube/GmuzUZTJ0GA?si=etakji2IrzXpeZok

Humility is key. The willful low position and
acknowledgment of ignorance is the correct approach. It's the right path upward or out.

"'Truly I tell you,' he said, 'unless you turn and become like little children, you will never enter the kingdom of heaven. Therefore, whoever humbles himself like this child—is the greatest in the kingdom of heaven.'" (Matthew 18:3-4 CSB).

Babies and children are little humans. They are not adults simply because of their small size but also because of their stage in development and maturity. There is an expectation to move from undeveloped to maturity.

One of the more helpful things I've learned in Bible study is that the different characters, themes and truths in the Bible function in multiple roles at the same time. This adds sophistication, complexity, depth and richness to the characters and story.

There is a theme of "the fool" in the Bible.

Throughout the Old Testament we are presented with characters, often who are playing dual roles. On the one hand they are playing a salvific role. It's a human ideal role for Israel and others to look up to. They are signifying the characteristics and traits of a master, a supreme human that should be emulated. This is in contrast to evil or others who aren't at their level. They play this role because it testifies to the one who is the eternal master. The one who is forever supreme, Jesus.

On the other hand, they are playing the role of the fool. This role identifies with their father, Adam. They fail. They fall short. This is in contrast to the true perfect master, the one to come, Jesus.

Adam introduced sin and death to humanity, Noah got drunk, Abraham lied, Moses murdered, David committed adultery, Solomon worshipped idols.

But God is using not just their successes but their failures to move the story forward toward the Messiah.

So, the theme is layered. You have characters in the role of master in contrast to the general population. At the same time those same characters are playing the role of fool in contrast to the coming Messiah.

This same pattern is true of Israel as a whole. God's chosen people are made holy by God in contrast to the rest of the nations. Yet, at the same time, Israel fails over and over again, playing the role of fool in contrast to God's only Begotten Son who is perfect. Jesus is the master in contrast to the trial and error of the characters throughout the Old Testament. He is Wisdom in contrast to the fool.

> Therefore, everyone who hears these words of mine and acts on them will be like a wise man who built his house on the rock. The rain fell, the rivers rose, and the winds blew and pounded that house, yet it didn't collapse, because its foundation was on the rock. But everyone who hears these words of mine and doesn't act on them will be like a foolish man who built his house on the sand. The rain fell, the rivers rose, the winds blew and pounded that house, and it collapsed with a great crash.—Matthew 7:24–27 (csb)

This theme is noted by Paul when he states in a letter to the Corinthian church,

> The first man Adam became a living being; The last Adam became a life-giving spirit. However, the spiritual is not first, but the natural, then the spiritual. The first man was from the earth, a man of dust; the second man is from heaven.—1 Corinthians 15:45 (csb)

This motif is central to God's plan of salvation; suffering and death first, then redemption and glory.

Are all kids deserving of a trophy?

If you don't know what failure is, how will you be able to adequately identify success, or know if or when things are right, good and better?

More than that, if you aren't willing to see and face your failure, then transformation, improvement, and salvation is lost altogether. Making temporal feelings and high self-esteem king leaves you delusional, undeveloped and hopeless.

So, comedy, or the comedian, is playing a particular role and has a particular function in narrative and life. The role is a fool as a forerunner to the savior.

This is where comedy is found, right in the middle of the suffering, the hardship, the trial.

Laughter lets us know that the pain is real, the failure is real, the loss is real, the awkwardness is real!! BUT, the road, the story doesn't end there!

The effect, pleasure, and love of comedy is what the supremacy of the logos feels like.

Comedians—We. Love. You!! We Need You!! Thank you for making us laugh.

> As it is written in Isaiah the prophet: See, I am sending my messenger ahead of you; he will prepare your way. A voice of one crying out in the wilderness: Prepare the way for the Lord; make his paths straight! John came baptizing in the wilderness and proclaiming a baptism of repentance for the forgiveness of sins. The whole Judean countryside and all the people of Jerusalem were going out to him, and they were baptizing by him in the Jordan River, confessing their sins. John wore a camel-hair garment with a leather belt around his waist and ate locusts and wild honey. He proclaimed, "One who is more powerful than I am is coming after me. I am not worthy to stoop down and untie the strap of his sandals. I baptize you with water, but he will baptize you with the Holy Spirit."—Mark 1:2–8 (csb)

The king who had John's head chopped off, actually liked John and desired the contrary to his demise. The King who was headed down to meet John by the water, placed his body into John's hands and allowed him to hold him under the drowning waters, trusting he would bring him back up again.

35
The Joker

Infinitude is at the bottom of the bottom. Right next to it is failure and pain. It just may be momentary optimism that is exuberantly expressing, "The story doesn't end here."

If infinitude is real, and suffering is a necessary part in the journey, who's to say that suffering won't begin to fill up the infinite amount of reality, your reality. It certainly seems to threaten in that direction.

That is more than enough to produce fear, bitterness, or resentment. At any moment, when encountering limitation, loss, suffering or evil, we have to decide how to respond. One of those options is certainly bitterness, resentment, and vengefulness.

The character of the Joker, in the Batman storyline, is a clown. Clowns play the role of the jester, or the comedian. They're meant to be happy, goofy, funny, and yet the Joker is a villain; dark, down, dangerous. What went wrong?

In the ancient script of the Bible, in the early pages of Genesis, there's a short story about two brothers, Cain and Abel. Cain gets called out for falling short and not being what he should be. Cain is a fool. But from what we learned above the fool is not the end but beginning.

Cain certainly has the opportunity to learn and do better, especially with both his brother and God present. Yet, Cain made a conscious decision about how to respond to his position and status. It was to turn downward. He became resentful and vengeful.

> We had Batman on one side, saying that Harvey Dent represents a good vision of what the city can become. And then we had the Joker on the other side, saying that any man can be corrupted and turned into a villain if you push him hard enough. And the Joker is kind of right...

—David Goyer, "How I Wrote The Dark Knight." YouTube Video, August 31, 2019, 14:01. https://youtu.be/yqlhU6hE14A?si=XRMkItN0CiT9S5WM

Lament with me, brother. Our Great Father is dead.—Scott, Ridley, director. Gladiator. Universal Pictures, DreamWorks Pictures, United International Pictures. 2000. 2h 35m.

Suffering and loss are a permanent fixture in life. There are actual reasons to be angry, upset, overwhelmed, confused and heartbroken. These elements are so large and sure that no positive attitude alone can withstand them. Humans know this. The frustration of being limited, the pain of losing, the shock and torment of malevolence, makes it not so obvious that the simple upward gaze will be a sure pathway out.

> Certainly, the most destructive vice, if you like, that a person can have, more than pride, which is supposedly the number one of the cardinal sins, is self-pity. Self-pity is the worst possible emotion anyone can have. And the most destructive. It is, to slightly paraphrase what Wilde said about hatred, and I think actually hatred's a subset of self-pity and not the other way around, It destroys everything around it, except itself.

> Self-pity will destroy relationships, it'll destroy anything that's good, it will fulfill all the prophecies it makes and leave only itself. And it's so simple to imagine that one is hard done by, and that things are unfair, and that one is underappreciated, and that if only one had had a chance at this, only one had had a chance at that, things would have gone better, you would be happier if only this, that one is unlucky. All those things. And some of them may well even be true. But, to pity oneself as a result of them is to do oneself an enormous disservice.—CyberDeadly, "Stephen Fry Discusses Self-Pity", YouTube Video, November 17, 2011, 2:14. YouTube Video. https://youtu.be/r_2kelqYz_o?si=hWNp3l5ZNPsUQUsy

The Joker, instead of accepting the brutality and frustration of life and using it as a means to point outward and upward, turns and chooses to make war on the entirety of life itself. Because if there is a good, that includes these elements in life that are so difficult and painful, the good doesn't deserve to be.

If your victim status is the justification for doing wrong, then you simultaneously justify the wrong done to you, because we are all victims. That justification just puts you into an infinite regress of guiltless perpetrators and hopeless victims.

No wonder Christianity in the West is weak, shallow and dormant: no one is at fault. We attribute blame to the other worldviews, denominations, religions, political party, and persons. Our argument of the doctrine of evil is the same as everyone else's, "It's them!" That is so anti-Christian, anti-the gospel, anti-true, that it's embarrassing.

When it's coming from Christian leaders who know how to state the points of the doctrine of sin but are hardly intimate with and able to articulate its complexities, nuances and darkness, it's quite alarming. The lack of sophistication is detrimental.

Human beings hold as much in common with one another as differences. If that's true then in any scenario, including the most evil, when you are observing another human, you should be keenly aware that you are observing yourself. Unfortunately, This falls on deaf ears in an individualistic saturated society.

Hell is real. How do I know? How do you know? Because the things that define it and make it up are present in micro ways all around us and in each of us. We have witnessed varying degrees of each element, and there is no indication that it cannot get worse. Infinitude runs in all directions, down is certainly one of them. This is the Joker's aim.

> You either die a hero or you live long enough to see yourself become the villain.—Nolan, Christopher director. *The Dark Knight*. USA: Warner Bros., Warner Bros. Pictures, FilmFlex, 2008. Film.

> This is actually one of my all-time favorite movie quotes. The reason I like it is not just because it sounds cool, but because it's the perfect illustration of Hegel's theory of evil.

He says, 'Evil Resides in the very gaze which perceives Evil all around itself.'

In other words, the best way to be evil is to think that you're fighting to promote good. So, evil isn't its own thing. Evil emerges from an over-commitment to wanting to eradicate evil. It's like, "The road to hell is paved with good intentions."—Julian de Medeiros, @themeaningproject, "This will always be the best Batman movie." Tiktok, August 11, 2021.

"The fear of the Lord is the beginning of wisdom."
—Proverbs 9:10 (csb)

It was silent. The construction, initiated by God, of the hierarchy, the house, the temple, the people, defined and built by law and tradition had become stale and corrupt. The journey out to a place worth pursuing and living, filled with abundance and promise, had led right into the powerful appetite of the devouring global empires. Seemingly no better than the position where it all began, back inside the stone walls of Egypt.

"The fool says in his heart, 'There's no God.'"
—Psalm 14:1 (csb)

THE SON: A FLU SHOT

Give a man a fish, feed him for a day. Teach a man to fish, feed him for a lifetime. —Old adage

....

36
An Introduction

> All of us like sheep have gone astray, we have turned, each one, to his own way; but the Lord has caused the wickedness of us all [our sin, our injustice, our wrongdoing] to fall on Him [instead of us]. He was oppressed and He was afflicted, Yet He did not open His mouth [to complain or defend Himself]; like a lamb that is led to the slaughter, and like a sheep that is silent before her shearers, so He did not open His mouth.—Isaiah 53:6–7 (amp)

> The chief priests accused him of many things. So again Pilate asked him, "Aren't you going to answer? See how many things they are accusing you of." But Jesus still made no reply, and Pilate was amazed.—Mark 15:3–5 (niv)

I was in love once. Is there anything better?

I wanted to be married by twenty-five. As I've gotten older it's become increasingly apparent to me that the reason I don't have a wife and kids is on me.

I used to chalk it up to God. "It's all in His timing, His plan, His orchestration, and His ordering the details to make it happen. God is sovereign after all." It certainly brought a level of relief. The sympathy and encouragement from others felt nice as well.

Yet, it hit me one day, God ain't coming for me. He's waiting on me. Am I who I should be? Have I done what I could?

That doesn't feel as good. That's not as easy to face. I'm responsible.

In biblical theology, there is a move from law to embodiment, from transcendent to incarnation, from word to action. That pattern is found in the nature of God, how we are engineered, how He unfolds the story in relating to us, how we are made right, and how we relate back to Him.

That is a lot. Let's begin here, with this question.

If God is triune, exactly why, among other things, is the second person, the Son, the one sent to suffer?

Each person of the Trinity is perfect in being and function for relating to the other two persons in the Godhead. You cannot and will not understand one of the persons without understanding their unique role in relation to the other two persons.

Every characteristic, down to the smallest detail defining each person, is present for relating to the other two persons.

When you are learning something in particular about one of the persons, you are also learning about the other two persons. Not only because they share characteristics, but also because of how they are different and are uniquely characterized, one for the other.

This is the general framework from which God creates our reality. Why would He do it any other way?

So what characterizes the second person, the Son?

If Francis Schaeffer is right about the fundamental nature of God being defined and infinite, then it becomes quite clear that those are opposing realities and would need a third element, if you will, to operate between and in relation to them.

In order to be considered or qualified as the supreme ideal and the remedy for humanity and the cosmos, you would have to have a particular nature. You would need to possess certain characteristics. You would require elements in being and function that would match the design of the intended targeted object.

The titles of supremacy and Savior don't get tacked on to something or someone and pass as true and right simply because of wishful thinking or fundamentalist dogmatism.

There would need to be a sophistication that matched the multi layered make up of humanity. It would need to reach so far back that it met at the point of intention for the cosmos. It would need to extend so far in the future that it was forever tied to hope.

The Supreme and Savior would also need to be tangible and accessible at the most subtle and potent points of human pain and experience; simple enough for anyone to reach out and grasp in order to be known.

More often than not we offer religious cliches as the aim and solution, without understanding what they mean. Because of this, they are separated from our actual world by a chasm so wide they aren't worth being the ideal or remedy. That says something about us, not about the nature of what is articulated in religious narrative.

> The thing that you should put in control is the bloody thing that pays attention and learns. Everything else in the hierarchy should be subordinate to the thing that pays attention and learns. And you can think, well that's the message of the idea of the logos, that's for sure. Because logos is partly attention and partly communication. And you learn a lot by communicating with others.—Jordan B. Peterson, "Lecture: biblical Series VI: The Psychology of the Flood." YouTube Video, July 3, 2017, 2:35:57. https://youtu.be/wNjbasba-Qw

I read a book in college titled *Plowing in Hope toward a Biblical Theology of Culture*. In part, it demonstrated that the scriptural narrative begins in a garden but ends with a garden city.

It assumed that the garden city was an update from just the garden. Now, if God is perfect and what He creates is perfect, then how could what He initially designed be improved?

The completed perfect structure isn't the ideal or aim. In part, because it doesn't take into account all of reality. Which includes what isn't known or what hasn't happened yet, infinitude essentially.

So, when structure bumps up against the infinite, it ends up falling apart. It's not able to fit in the overwhelming aspect of the chaotic infinite.

What becomes the ideal, then, is the entity that is able to create and restructure in the face of the infinite, including worst-case scenarios. The description of that ideal is Christ.

This is the story that is constantly being told at varying levels of analysis throughout the Bible: Noah in the ark, Abraham into a new land, Joseph into Egypt, Moses into the wilderness, Joshua conquering the promised land, David stepping out and facing the enemies; these are leaders, navigators, mediators, problem solvers. They are living beings. Not stone structures. Not merely ideas or dreams.

Because the element of infinitude is permanent, there is no structure that can be built that will not always need to be updated to face the fact that it will essentially grow old and become irrelevant. There is always more.

The proper mode of being, the highest value then, should be one that is able to build a new and improved structure with the ever-present new information.

It's more than that, though.

If there was a perfect structure constructed with the highest standard and strictest boundaries and was up against the epitome of open and infinite, which included the darkest opposing threats, then the entity that had to be present to mediate between both, would have to bear the complete weight of the structure. It would have to meet its every expectation and fulfill the debt of any failure at any point.

It would have to face the chaotic infinite with all of its darkest strongest potentials and be able to overcome them. Then it would have to be able to come out on the other side with a structure able to be lived in and related to.

The reality of aim, boundaries, and structure itself is eternal and good. It is always present but never alone. The reality of the infinite, in its potential and beckoning for life to continue is eternal and good. It's always present but is never alone. Each needs the other, and the third element that brings them together and forever keeps them together is the mediator, the sacrificial agent, and the conquering hero.

Christ is the living entity that is eternally subject to the structure, faces the infinite, and comes out living, updated, and able to move forward.

This is the framework for the cosmos, the blueprint for human reality.

We are made in the image of this trinity. We are rightly united to this entity, Christ, for salvation and eternal life because this Christ functions and operates properly at the most fundamental level of what reality is. Jesus is the image of the invisible God.

37
The Seed and Embodiment

From thought to speech.
    From speech to action.
From conceptual to actual.
From informed to involved.
From walled city to exploration.
From father and mother to wife.
From invisible to visible.
From spirit to flesh.
From law to obedience.
From heaven to earth.

I hope to have kids one day. For now, I have the great joy of being "Uncle Buddy" to my nieces and nephews.

Kids are the best. They come from you. They reflect you. They are brand-new humans. They're small and full of energy. Everything is new, instantaneous, and dramatic. They help us remember what it's like to experience life for the first time.

If you pause and take note, in the Bible narrative, throughout history and in modern day, there is a deep, dark theme of a vicious assault on babies and children.

Why?

Who and what God is and how He functions, is not changed once He creates the cosmos and begins history. Creating is directly in line with and flowing out of His fundamental nature.

He creates something outside of Himself. He then relates to and dwells with His creation. This is right in line with who God is and how He functions within the Trinity eternally all by Himself.

The Son is the eternal, constant image, exact imprint of, exact representation of the nature of God.

The Father is structured and defined. The Spirit is out and about choosing what is always good and patterned after the Father. The Son, then, is sent by the Father, out to where the Holy Spirit has led and marked out. He resides there, bringing the Father forward into the new to reestablish. This is the storyline of the Christian Scriptures.

When the Son is birthed into human history in male human form, it's only fitting that He embodies the creation, which was patterned perfectly after the transcendent. Now, live and in living color for humankind to observe, document, and relate to, the second person of the Trinity houses the fullness of God, subject to the Father and led by the Spirit.

In the beginning God created by speaking, using words. What is produced by His words is actual space and matter, and it's called good.

John, in the New Testament, calls Jesus the Word. Word that becomes flesh. He is sent from the Father, sets up shop in the created order and acts in a perfected manner. It is basically demonstrating that what God has made, is indeed patterned after, for, and about him. It deserves to be forever.

This demonstration of the Word being the means by which the created order is worked out and carried forward in a proper manner, is being demonstrated all throughout the unfolding story of the scripture.

God gives Noah the precise accurate instructions to build a boat to weather the storm. He gives Solomon the instructions on how to build an actual structure patterned after the heavenly home of God so that humans and God can relate in actual time and space through that structure.

When Jesus arrives, He is the embodiment of the explanation given throughout the Old Testament. He is the precise demonstration of the explanation that becomes the actual means and passageway by which the human and creation can find remedy, transformation, and continuous life.

It's a strange thing . . . that one of the things we already agreed on, as far as I can tell, is that the antidote to pathological dogmatism is free truthful expression . . . One of the things I would say is absolutely crucial to Christianity, in particular is the notion that the thing that's redeeming is exactly that, and . . . it's a universal truth. Now, if we both agree on that, the idea that the free expression of truthful speech is the antidote, let's say, to both nihilism and to totalitarianism, then the notion that that might be embodied in something like the Word, which is truly, I think the deepest of Christian ideas, how is that not the same claim? Now, let me elaborate on it a little more completely. So, here's a strange thing . . . This notion that redemption is to be found in truthful speech, is actually embodied in Christian mythology, let's say, as a personality and not as an idea. It's actually something that you embody and act out. It's not just an idea. And that's why there's an emphasis on the idea of the embodiment of the Word in Flesh. It's a very sophisticated idea. I mean it's an insanely sophisticated idea.—Jordan Peterson. Pangburn. "Sam Harris vs Jordan Peterson | God, Atheism, The Bible, Jesus—Part 1—Presented by Pangburn." YouTube Video, 2:06:37. August 31, 2018. https://youtu.be/jey_CzIOfYE

The seed is the entity which holds the essence and nature of its united source, like a fully developed tree, for example. It then develops and/or acts out that nature. What the source is, becomes actualized, and made manifest.

The seed of a tree contains all of the elements and nature of the particular tree that it came from, but also, everything that tree-ness is. The seed contains the actuality, or the demonstration of what tree-ness is. It becomes the passageway by which trees will continue to be. It carries all of the necessary elements.

Jesus is the seed, The Son.

All the peoples on earth will be blessed through you and your offspring.—Genesis 28:14 (csb)

The promises were spoken to Abraham and to his seed. Scripture does not say 'and to seeds,' meaning many people, but 'and to your seed,' meaning one person, who is Christ.—Galatians 3:16 (niv)

For to us a child is born, to us a son is given, and the

government will be on his shoulders. And he will be called Wonderful Counselor, Mighty God, Everlasting Father... —Isaiah 9:6 (niv)

He is the exact living image [the essential manifestation] of the unseen God [the visible representation of the invisible], the firstborn [the preeminent one, the sovereign, and the originator] of all creation. For by Him all things were created in heaven and on earth, [things] visible and invisible, whether thrones or dominions or rulers or authorities; all things were created and exist through Him [that is, by His activity] and for Him. And He Himself existed and is before all things, and in Him all things hold together. [He is the controlling, cohesive force of the universe.]

—Colossians 1:15–17 (amp)

This passage is not just telling us that Jesus is eternal, and not just that He is the one behind the reality of the universe, but also the fact, that the universe is and how it is, is directly tied to who and what Jesus is, how He functions eternally as the second person in the trinity.

God, having spoken to the fathers long ago in [the voices and writings of] the prophets in many separate revelations [each of which set forth a portion of the truth], and in many ways, has in these last days spoken [with finality] to us in [the person of One who is by His character and nature] His Son [namely Jesus], whom He appointed heir and lawful owner of all things, through whom also He created the universe [that is, the universe as a space-time-matter continuum]. The Son is the radiance and only expression of the glory of [our awesome] God..., and the exact representation and perfect imprint of His [Father's] essence... —Hebrews 1:1–3 (amp)

The Seed, the Son is the eternal actualization and embodiment of God and also the passageway by which God continues to be.

So, in the trinity, the Son is eternally the representation of the invisible and the one who plays the role of making new and inhabiting the new.

He is also playing that role in relation to God's creation and unfolding plan in relation to creation. He images God perfectly as human by being the seed of the human, in contrast to the fallen human. He becomes the passageway by which the union between God and human is rectified and able to continue forever.

The Seed, the Son, is willing and able to bear the weight of the law, meeting its requirements, and walk toward the harshest and darkest elements of reality because he is the perfected embodiment of the union between Father and the Spirit.

"The seed of the woman . . ." will be the one to contend with the Evil Serpent. The corruption of God's created reality, demands one to enter into it embodied, then be positioned and able to contend with its troubles.

"For this reason a man shall leave his father and his mother, and shall be joined to his wife."—Genesis 2:24 (amp).

Why is the second person of the Trinity masculine/male?

The fullness of God, the union of Father and Spirit, dwelling in the God man, stands as one facing the open landscape and multiplicity of humanity, signified by the feminine, and chooses among them some to make His bride.

The Son takes on the form of the invisible God, pushing out from what could not be heard, seen, touched, and now present to relate and function in a human earthly manner. It demonstrates in completion that what God is and what he has created is in sync.

Man is made in the image and likeness of God. Jesus is the image of the Invisible God, the second Adam. The perfected, full representation of the one true deity in embodied form, demonstrating for all creation, that we are about and for God. What we are and how we are is precisely linked to who and what God is.

The Son is the eternal being that represents the priority of the good, dwelling forever new. God is worth continuing, and he demonstrates that by being one who reproduces Himself forever.

The result of the perfectly defined and the infinite, joining in good will, appreciation, and commitment, is life continued. It produces an entity that is composed of concise definition and able to move into and contend with the unknown infinite, eternally.

> That knowledge or understanding in God which we must conceive of as first is His knowledge of everything possible. That love which must be this knowledge is what we must conceive of as belonging to the essence of the Godhead in its first subsistence. Then comes a reflex act of knowledge and His viewing Himself and knowing Himself and so knowing His own knowledge and so the Son is begotten. There is such a thing in God as knowledge of knowledge, an idea of an idea. Which can be nothing else than the idea or knowledge repeated.
>
> The world was made for the Son of God especially. For God made the world for Himself from love to Himself; but God loves Himself only in a reflex act. He views Himself and so loves Himself, so He makes the world for Himself viewed and reflected on, and that is. The same with Himself repeated or begotten in His own idea, and that is His Son. When God considers of making any thing for Himself, He presents Himself before Himself and views Himself as His End, and that viewing Himself is the same as reflecting on Himself or having an idea of Himself, and to make the world for the Godhead thus viewed and understood is to make the world for the Godhead begotten and that is to make the world for the Son of God.—Edwards, Jonathan. *Writings on the Trinity, Grace, and Faith*. Sang Hyun Lee, Editor. USA: Yale University Press. 2008. 141–42.

Nothing could be more profound and exciting than having children. As routine as it is in the human experience, it's brand-new every time, and especially for parents.

The prenatal and newborn infant is certainly a human made in God's image. But the fetus and baby are also analogous to the second person of the trinity. The baby is a pattern, always demonstrating the role of the eternal God and Son.

So, a baby is reflective of the nature of God and the Son. Not just in being human, but in being a baby.

Reproduction culminates in human offspring. The human culmination is rooted in the nature of God as one who reproduces eternally in the person of Christ.

The newborn baby, in contrast to a clone, is a reflection of the eternal pattern of the Son's relation to the union of Father and Holy Spirit.

The prenatal, infant, baby is the earthly representation of the profound goodness of the eternal Son. A baby is a type of Christ.

"Whoever welcomes one of these little children in my name welcomes me" (Mark 9:37 niv).

"Jesus said, "Let the little children come to me, and do not hinder them, for the kingdom of heaven belongs to such as these" (Matthew 19:14 niv).

"Children are a heritage from the Lord, offspring a reward from Him" (Psalm 127:3 niv).

Assault on babies and children then, is Satanic by definition.

That Christ would enter human history as a prenatal and newborn baby is the essence of redemption. Not just because it affirms the value of humanity made in Gods image, but because it pronounces the pattern of baby that matches his nature as eternal Son.

38

The Willful Sufferer

Intentionally stepping into the darkness.
Deciding to bear the burden.
Voluntarily choosing the pain.
Welcoming the difficulty.

> Change is undesirable to most because the chisel is painful but is needed to sculpt the future. So, embrace the process. The pain only lasts for a short time, but the results will last a lifetime.—Matthew Ruggiero (reddye40), Xsport Fitness," Instagram, December 17, 2019. https://www.instagram.com/p/B6MatrChXwZ/

Just about all true inspirational quotes you have ever encountered include facing difficulty, suffering, and darkness as a good thing.

> God has set down some universal principles for how elements of His creation grow and mature. One particular important principle is what developmental psychologists call the zone of proximal development. Sounds impressive, doesn't it? And it is – although we prefer to think of it simply as "the zone." This principle says that anything that grows and matures does best when provided with the right mixture of two critical ingredients: support and challenge.—Dr. Tim Clinton and Dr. Gary Sibcy, *Attachments: Why You Love, Feel, and Act the Way You Do.* (Nashville: Thomas Nelson, 2009), 133.

Avoiding difficulty or going in the opposite direction of it, is not the answer.

This isn't peripheral, one of many means; it is the fundamental to what we know about living and thriving. It's no accident that Christianity has at its central developed explanation, a tortured, suffering human.

In order for a tree to be, a seed has to be buried in the ground.

In order for muscle to build it has to be ripped and broken down.

In order to become proficient in any field, any craft, any skill, you must be subject to conditioning, training, discipline and work.

Freedom isn't had by the absence of rule and boundary, but by the willingness to be subject to and mastered by them.

Stepping out, trial and error, is the only path forward.

Going hand in hand with the concept of embodiment is the operation of the will to suffer.

The movement from an inward conceptual idea, led by the mind and emotions, now has to get pushed out and worked out in real time and space by the will. It's a decision to turn and face the unknown and difficulty, engage it and wrestle with it.

Instant vs. Process

A lot of criticism toward, and confusion about God, I think, is in and around this concept of instant versus process.

The first criticism sounds like, "God cannot actually know that much. He's not that powerful. His ability for control can't be that great. Miracles, the supernatural and so on, I can't believe that."

There is a misunderstanding or denial that God is all powerful, all knowing, and in control of all. Therefore, there is "reason" to disbelieve.

On the flip side, and oftentimes at the same time or from the same persons, there is criticism of God's seeming limitations.

If God is all knowing, if God is all powerful, if God is in control, then why doesn't He do it, do it right, or better, and do it now?

In fact, if we pushed that further, you could ask questions like; why didn't Eve give birth to Jesus? Jesus could have gone back into the garden, crushed the serpent's head, gone back out, gotten His parents, brought them back into the garden, and called it a day.

Why the entire Old Testament with its hundreds and thousands of years?

That's great that God brought his people out of slavery in Egypt. But He is the one who leads them there. Couldn't He have provided food for Jacob and his family during the famine, so they didn't have to end up in Egypt in the first place?

When you are justified by placing your faith in Jesus, why are you not sanctified and glorified at the same time? Why an entire life of defeat, struggle, and sin?

I think the answer is simple. Our concept of God is wrong or lacking. The reality of process, time, or working out, are rooted in what God is. In fact, these elements are required in order to be a living being.

So, when God who is all powerful, all knowing, and in control of all, states that He is working all things out for your good, and it isn't instantaneous, but includes time, strain, struggle and pain, He is showing you Himself by using the element of process, as such, which finds its origin in Himself.

The will inside of the inner being of the human sits between the mind and emotions and takes what is inward and pushes it out into action.

There's a reason the Old Testament isn't enough. There has to be a move from written law or stated standard, to flesh and blood.

To suffer willfully, means to intentionally act out in subjection to a standard and work out in space, contending with all possibilities of action to harness a particular set of actions.

If you do not intentionally, willfully step out into suffering, the suffering will come to you and overtake you. If you intentionally act to avoid and move away from suffering, you will never develop, grow, or be strengthened to be better and equipped for the ever-present threats or reality of more.

God is the highest standard and always beckons forward into the infinite.

All of the weightlifting gurus, Arnold Schwarzenegger included, tell you that it's not simply going through the motion of lifting weight;

you have to lean into it. The point is to focus on the muscle to rip and tear it. The point is to feel the burn. That's how you get results. The point is suffering.

All of these people, sales reps, and products, trying to motivate you to work out by making it as easy as possible. That defeats the purpose!

Growth or everlasting life, does not occur simply by accommodation or eliminating borders. It most often comes through work or voluntary suffering.

But why?

More can be experienced, often in quick easy fashion, but the goal is to remain being, ideally in a good way, after more becomes a part of you. The reality is finitude up against infinitude with no walls or door will be overtaken and consumed by the infinite.

On the flip side, if the finite has only structure with no windows, doors, and all possible passageways in or out sealed off permanently, then the result will be stagnation and death.

Being open, liberal, extroverted, charismatic, or artistic means that you value and emphasize the need to move away from strict boundaries and tradition. In order to continue to live, if living and being are good, then this open aspect of being has to be a fundamental element, and always present.

If, however, the definition of reality is dominated or only understood with this open mode of being, it will consume and devour and bring things to an end. Infinitude is too much, too wide, too deep, too powerful, too chaotic to be the stand-alone description of reality.

You can't walk into the gym and just determine that you are going to lift the heaviest weights in any fashion you desire. It will crush you and injure you severely.

The structural finite mode of being, like the conservative, traditional, the known, the past means that you value what is organized, planned, productive, safe, secure, and understood. This is the value of remaining inside, moving away from threat, what's different, and what's unknown. In order for being to continue, then this mode of being has to be present, valued and utilized, because the danger of infinitude is absolutely real.

But, if you are too conservative and decide not to work out your body out of fear of injury and pain, or out of lack of desire for change and growth, it will lead to illness, weakness, and death.

These two modes of being, need to be present and accommodated at the same time. Yet you have to be able to navigate through the ever-present challenge of each of their downsides.

The Son, or all things patterned after the Son, sit, operate and function in this role, ever mediating between the two.

Of course, in the nature of the persons of the trinity, there is no downside or shadow. Each is complete and fully God.

Conservatism wants to remain. Liberalism wants to progress.

If you remain, you get stuck with both the elements that are good and with the ones that aren't. You deny a fundamental aspect of reality, namely that there is far more than what is or what has been. You will be stuck, fixed, enslaved, turned to stone and cease to be alive.

If you progress, neglecting and despising the known and the tradition, moving out into the infinite unknown; you will be both unable to decipher the benefit of any particular element out of the infinite number of options. You will be ill-equipped to face and withstand the worst overpowering elements that are fit to shred you to pieces.

Refusal to progress is not an option. Refusal to remain in the confines of hierarchy is not an option.

Subjecting to the constraint of aiming at the Most-High, and always pushing away from the current state to contend with the always more to be closer to the Most High is the human's design. Both must be embodied at the same time.

Jesus embodies the finite and living human form, takes on the full weight of the Father's standards and their judgments. He contends with the darkest villains, in death and evil that plague the human reality at the deepest and most profound levels.

The willingness to face these worst aspects of reality honestly, boldly and with an aim toward the highest, actually provides the means to overcome them. Death certainly plays a role but becomes the passageway to transformation. Essentially the figure is made greater having contended with such forces.

"Then Jesus said to them, 'O foolish men, and slow of heart to trust and believe in everything that the prophets have spoken! Was it not necessary for the Christ to suffer these things and [only then to] enter His Glory?'"—Luke 24:25–26 (amp)

This description and storyline of reality is found at multiple levels of our living experience, and certainly at the greatest and highest conceptual levels in the religious domain.

These aren't just arbitrary, outdated ideas. This is what actually works. This is what is most meaningful. It's rooted so deeply and concretely, that it's found in what is most fundamental, the concept and being of God Himself.

So, what is the message that should always remain and be held as the highest authority? This message. What being should remain across all of time and held as the highest among the highest? This Being!

> What happens in the most profound of such texts is, the idea that the process by which your knowledge is updated has to occupy a position in the hierarchy of values that supersedes your reliance on dogma, is the fundamental claim. That's why, for example, in Christianity the notion is that the Word is the highest of values. And that's embodied Word, and that's the thing that mediates between Order and Chaos, and everything else has to be subject to that.—Pangburn. "Sam Harris vs Jordan Peterson | God, Atheism, The Bible, Jesus—Part 1—Presented by Pangburn." YouTube Video. 2:06:37. August 31, 2018.
>
> https://youtu.be/jey_CzIOfYE

Sitting between the Father and the Spirit and contending with their differences seems to be directly tied to suffering being the correct pathway forward.

The aim of Satan tempting Jesus in the desert was to try and get Jesus to bypass the cross. To skip the suffering.

John Ortberg makes a similar point in a message on Esther and facing your shadow,

> I think the shadow mission for Jesus was to be the leader without suffering. Was to be the Messiah without a cross. F. F. Bruce, great New Testament scholar, said, "time and time again, the temptation came from many directions, to choose some less costly way of fulfilling His calling than the way of suffering and death." Time after time...
>
> a less costly way. And you know in the desert the evil one tempts Him to achieve his mission without hunger. "Turn these stones to bread, you don't need to be hungry." Without pain, "Throw yourself down from the temple, the angels will bear you up." Without opposition, "Bow down before me and all the kingdoms of the earth will be yours."—Gracebibleonline, "John Ortberg—A Leader's Greatest Fear—2007 Leadership Summit", YouTube Video. May 18, 2021. 1:00:58. https://youtu.be/fv-HzdS2JGk?si=Jc-ptofsrZAVOz50

There isn't a position or mode of being, anywhere, at any time, that doesn't have a shadow directly tied to it.

We think that the darkness and evil aspects are something separated from the good. That is only part of the explanation. They are uniquely tied to the good like what a shadow is to an object. This makes the work of pursuing the good and defeating evil that much more sophisticated. It won't happen by accident. Good demands strain, struggle, and suffering.

The reality of taking responsibility is at the heart of matter, the matter, and all that matters.

If your primary plan of action is to run from, denounce or demonize a particular structure or mode of being that is rooted eternally as good, because it has been corrupted by its shadow, you have not taken full stock of the complexity of the situation. In other words, you are being critical but not critical enough, and the result of that may be fatal or hellish.

The spirit of Cain speaks to Jesus in the desert, "You've lowered yourself enough. You have suffered enough. You have felt the restriction of limitation enough. You have the right to lift yourself up and make yourself the first. Eliminate the judge, remove the standard and ignore it. This is all there is, so just make the most out of what you can, now. make your own way."

Cain is the shadow. Christ is the master because he faces the restriction and His enemies. This is the pathway of suffering.

The Father's law is as strict and demanding as it gets. The Spirit's freedom is as vast and overwhelming as can be. The Son operates constantly bearing the weight of order and facing the strain of infinitude. The only way to be and to continue to be is by the process of death and rebirth. It's by constantly shedding, sacrificing, and removing what is old, stale and unfit. It's painful. It takes time. It's difficult. It's complex. But in order to live, you have to accept and value death.

The pursuit of freedom without the presence and value of structure and authority will only be met by forces, circumstances and realities that overwhelm and overtake you.

Authority and structure without the pursuit of freedom will only produce tyranny and enslavement.

The proper mode of being is the willful subjection to authority, discipline, process, conditioning and death that is aimed out and forward; transforming you into an entity that is fit to contend with all that the infinite unknown has and the ability to restructure altogether.

The Son demonstrates this at the highest conceptual level. He willfully submits to the highest authority, constrained by the strictest rules and standards. He is led to face the darkest and fiercest oppositions. The end result is that he is transformed and fit to function and take on anything at any time, literally.

This concept, of willfully giving yourself to suffering, pain, hardship, trial, enslavement, for the aim of transcending and overcoming it, is worthy of attention. The way it is played out as a concept by the story of Jesus, on its own, deserves to be held as the highest of concepts realized, ever.

The fact that it's explained, not just as a concept, but as being embodied and acted out in real time and space by a person, is a demonstration that the highest and best concept, being pushed down and out through will and action is the correct process. It's good. It's beautiful. It's right. It's how God functions at the most fundamental level. It's a picture and demonstration of His nature.

The one who embodies the concept and follows the lead of the spirit into the future perfectly, deserves worship, in real time and space. This is the role Jesus plays, not just from God to Man, but eternally with God Himself.

Perhaps the reason that you aren't bowing down to this God and one called Jesus, other than the fact that you haven't had him explained to you before, is because it's the same reason you avoid taking responsibility for other areas in your life that are weak, broken, lacking, wrong and filthy. It's too difficult to face, too uncomfortable to walk through, too demanding and burdensome to take on.

When Jesus states, "Why do you look at the [insignificant] speck that is in your brother's eye, but do not notice and acknowledge the [egregious] log that is in your own eye?" (Matthew 7:3 ampc), maybe one of the reasons is because we are avoiding the pain of dealing with our own problems. And/or have to face the reality that we aren't equipped to remedy the problem.

Confession—which is agreeing with the highest standard of good about what you deserve for your failure and corruption, and believing that who Jesus is, how He functions, and what He has accomplished as the highest reality, concept, and mode of being, namely His willingness to suffer—demands that you not only think this, but admit it out loud, embody it, and live it out.

Why would anyone want to do that? It's much easier to be resentful, bitter, lazy, play the blame game, eat, drink, and be merry.

But you know in the deepest part of you, it would be wrong. It wars against your soul. You side with the worst of reality with that attitude and conscious view. You make things worse.

The spirit of Cain and the Joker, are always present, coaxing us toward hell, the denial of responsibility and away from the upward climb toward the kingdom of God.

"For whoever wants to save his life will lose it, but whoever loses his life because of me will find it."—Matthew 16:25 (csb)

The paradox! The pathway to hell is the denial of responsibility and acknowledgment that you deserve it. The road to the kingdom is through accepting the fact that you need to face hell and enter it.

> If your right eye causes you to sin, gouge it out and throw it away. For it is better that you lose one of the parts of your body than for your whole body to be thrown into hell. And if your right hand causes you to sin, cut it off and throw it away. For it is better that you lose one of the parts of your body than for your whole body to go into hell.—Matthew 5:29–30 (csb)

Theologian John Piper states that the essence of this passage is to suffer whatever you must to move away from the hellish and toward the kingdom of God. . . . Suffer whatever you must.

> Rather, blessed are those who hear the word of God and keep it.—Luke 11:28 ((csb)
>
> Do not merely listen to the word, and so deceive yourselves. Do what it says. Anyone who listens to the word but does not do what it says is like someone who looks at his face in a mirror and, after looking at himself, goes away and immediately forgets what he looks like. But whoever looks

intently into the perfect law that gives freedom and continues in it—not forgetting what they have heard but doing it—they will be blessed in what they do.—James 1:22-25 (niv)

So faith without deeds is dead.—James 2:26 (niv)

Whoever wants to be my disciple must deny themselves and take up their cross and follow me.—Matthew 16:24 (niv)

If you love me, keep my commands.—John 14:15 (niv)

No Pain, No Gain.
In *Attachments,* Clinton and Sibcy state,

> Because pain may be involved, practicing the disciplines requires courage, the willingness to endure the necessary cost to achieve something far better. When we avoid necessary pain, we only invite unnecessary anguish later. As Carl Jung counseled, all neurotic suffering, or unnecessary pain, is caused by the avoidance of legitimate pain.—Dr. Tim Clinton and Dr. Gary Sibcy, *Attachments: Why You Love, Feel, and Act the Way You Do.* (Nashville: Thomas Nelson, 2009), 164.

Jesus turned and walked into the horror and pain. Because He chose to face judgment and shame, it led Him to transcend and overcome it.

Jesus is the door by which we pass from weak to strong, death to life. Not arbitrarily, but because He is the prototype and archetype of transformation as such.

Confession and repentance are the hinge on which the door of salvation swings.

Facing the darkness within, contending with the evil rooted inside, and siding with the good to rid ourselves of the evil is faith in who and what Jesus is. Faith is the alignment with the being that is truest, which includes facing the best and the worst elements of being.

"For it pleased the Father for all the fullness [of deity—the sum total of His essence, all His perfection, powers, and attributes] to dwell [permanently] in Him (the Son), and through [the intervention of] the Son to reconcile all things to Himself, making Peace [with believers]" How? "... through the blood of His cross."

—Colossians 1:19–20 (amp)

Jesus depicts the reality of death and rebirth, ultimately, as the proper path eternally in relation to the trinity, as well as in God's relating to the human and his creation. It is this pattern, at the heart of the Son's position and function, that the created cosmos demonstrates at multiple levels, in varying degrees, and that we find at the pinnacle of meaning.

If Jesus is what the claim is that He is, it has to be an explanation that resonates far beyond the scope of the religious. In fact, part of what makes something religious is that it resonates through the differing disciplines and studies that make up the world and human beings.

This certainly is true for Jesus being the one who suffered ultimately.

"Anyone who wishes to understand Christ's words and to savor them fully should strive to become like him in every way."—Thomas à Kempis, *The Imitation of Christ*. (Holy Roman Empire: 1418–1427), 20.

The title of Thomas à Kempis' classic work is *The Imitation of Christ*. The whole point is to move from viewing and understanding, to embodiment and working out. That's the role that Jesus plays eternally and in the salvation plan. By necessity it is how we demonstrate our faith and belief that that is true.

"Difficulties strengthen the mind, as labor does the body."—Lucius Annaeus Seneca

39
The Mediator

The highest principle and ultimate solution must be both present and infinite.

If there is only provision for the moment, then it's not enough. If there is an endless supply of provision with no means for it to be reached, then it has no actual benefit.

If God only treated us like an infant and provided our every need in every moment, He would be relating to us as something less than human. Because we are made in His image and He is a self-sufficient being, He rightly designed and relates to us by placing us in the tension between the present and infinite. This requires training and learning as fundamental elements of our humanity. Training and learning reflect the nature of the second person of the Trinity as the mediator between the moment and the eternal.

If your highest principle is only present in theory, imagination, philosophical ideas, or feelings and doesn't know your name, isn't grounded in fact, can't bleed for you, then it's just a mirage. If your immediate helps, like money, relationships, entertainment, or career aren't tied to an objective higher principle that works across time for all time, then you truly aren't progressing.

If your ultimate solution cannot meet you where you are and take you where you need to go always, then it's not worthy of being named King of kings and Savior of the world.

Jesus is the mediator between man and God, the finite and infinite, the moment and the eternal because He Himself is the present transcendent.

He is uniquely fit to remedy the disintegration that sin causes in the human soul by reconnecting man to the one who is present infinite, the triune God of the Bible.

"For God was pleased to have all his fullness dwell in him, and through him to reconcile everything to himself, whether things on earth or things in heaven, by making peace . . ."—Colossians 1:19–20 (CSB)

"For to us a Child shall be born, to us a Son shall be given; And the government shall be upon His shoulder, and His name shall be called Wonderful Counselor, Mighty God, Everlasting Father, Prince of Peace. There shall be no end to the increase of His government and of peace"—Isaiah 9:6–7 (amp).

God is three persons. There is no personhood without communication.

Communication is about relating or being in a relationship. Communication is the element of reality that mediates between persons.

John states in his gospel that the essence of communication is rooted in and defined by what the second person of the trinity, the Son, is.

"In the beginning was the Word, and the Word was with God and the Word was God. He was with God in the beginning. All things were created through him, and apart from him not one thing was created that has been created"—John 1:1–3 (csb).

In the beginning God created the heavens and the earth. Now the earth was formless and empty, darkness covered the surface of the watery depths, and the Spirit of God was hovering over the surface of the waters. Then God said . . ."—Genesis 1:1–3 (csb).

Jesus is the Word, reason, logic or explanation, who is accurately revealing what is as well as creating that which will be good and able to be lived in, amidst the chaotic unknown. He perfectly images or reflects the Father and follows the lead of the Spirit to be the proper place to dwell in.

It's the favorable alarming word to Noah, to craft a boat out of wood, accurately and successfully for him to be inside and stay, literally, safely, while the world around him falls prey to the climactic collapse of dysfunction and chaos.

It's the prompting, authoritative word that picks up the man, Abram, leading him to leave his livelihood and trek through foreign lands to claim a living space that God has promised. A place where God would choose to live with humankind once again.

It's the intellectual, educated word that inspires Solomon, the king of Israel, to build a temple. It would be an actual structure, erected in the city where God would be present, accessible to the people. A place where everything that corrupts, clouds, and condemns would be dealt with and handled.

The Word is forming and creating space so that in the middle of chaos and trouble, life is present, light is present, future is present, meaning is present. It's a space where God and man can live together.

Articulated truth is a reflection of what is eternally worthy of trust. It's what is able to provide a path to follow or structure to be inside, no matter the circumstances. This is a description of what Jesus is and how He functions.

Let's bring back the brain. We stated above that the brain is divided into two hemispheres, order and chaos, functioning in two very different ways. Each of those differences match the fundamental difference of the Father and the Holy Spirit, which is the fundamental difference in the cosmos. But what of the Son?

Let me introduce you to the corpus callosum. What is the corpus callosum? I'm glad you asked. The name is Latin for "tough body."

> The brain is divided into the right and left hemisphere, and the corpus callosum connects the two halves. This bundle of nerve tissue contains over 200 million axons (nerve fibers that carry electrical impulses from neurons' cell bodies) by rough estimate. This neural tissue facilitates communication between the two sides of the brain.—The Healthline Editorial Team, medically reviewed by Seunggu Han, M.D., "Corpus Callosum of The Brain", *Healthline.com*, January 4, 2022. https://www.healthline.com/human-body-maps/corpus-callosum

The significant position and function of the corpus callosum is what the supremacy of the logos looks like.

"And in Him all things hold together. [His is the controlling, cohesive force of the universe.]"

—Colossians 1:17 (amp)

Jesus is the mediator between God and man as taught by Christian theology because it's His role eternally in the triune God.

40
The Truth: Round Two

What exactly is the truth again? Depending on who you are talking to, you may receive different answers.

If you can't agree on the nature of truth, you will have an even tougher time trying to agree on what is true.

Truth: strictest, strongest standard of definition.

Truth: infinite, never ending, always more to it.

There is no one thing, small or great, that literally, all of humanity from all of history knows everything about.

There is always more knowledge to be gained and understood about any one thing and everything.

D. A. Carson in an article on Postmodernism, put it like this,

> "Postmodernism articulates what we should have known but what modernism made difficult to see, namely, that there is more to human knowing than rationality, proofs, evidences, and linear thought." He continues a few paragraphs later, "In reality, as pre-modern epistemology understood, we may know some true things but never in an omniscient manner; we may know that certain things are objectively true but never with the absolute certainty according to God alone."—D. A. Carson, "the Dangers and Delights of Postmodernism", *Modern Reformation*, July/August 2003. https://www.modernreformation.org/resources/articles/the-dangers-and-delights-of-postmodernism#:~:text=For%20some%2C%20it%20evokes%20all,%2C%20and%9

If that is true, what are we to make of that?

We can certainly agree that God is infinite. So, the knowledge, or true things related to him are infinite. There is no point that we will reach in knowledge, understanding, and experience that will be exhausted related to God.

You can know something truly, accurately, rightly, but you will never know all related to it. Truth is both an accurate definition and never ending. It's open ended.

How could the bedrock of our understanding and knowledge be a paradox?

I think humans constantly oscillate between definitions of truth being both fixed and absolute, and being open and infinite, without ever realizing that both are correct. We oscillate on our concept of truth on grand scales.

In the West in the last one hundred years or so we have moved from modernity to postmodernity. This shift can, in part but significantly, be tied to our relationship and understanding of truth. We've moved from truth being strict and absolute, to truth being open and relative.

It's a constant negotiation between the fundamental reality of the nature of truth being both understood in strict order, law, and definition and it being open ended, not ever completely closed and finished.

Truth isn't a finalized, carved in stone, locked, throw away the key, reality. Nor is it a transient, ungraspable, momentary whim or feeling. Truth is what carries both of those.

Truth is a vehicle, perhaps a being or personality that lives within what is strict, what is accurately defined, and yet moves with it, carrying it forward.

It takes what is absolute and makes something new and good with it. It is always updating, creating, and re-creating. That can't be done without absolute objective reality. It can't happen without the infinite future being real. It can't happen without a mediating agent who consciously and willfully acts in perfect balance between the two.

Truth is valuing both paradoxical elements to the point of relating to both in perfect harmony. It would require a very particular extremely sophisticated entity to be able to manage such a role.

How do you spot the truth in any room you step into? It will be the thing that is most nuanced, strictly aligned with reality, and open ended to what isn't yet, both at the same time.

Truth isn't facts. Facts aren't the truth because they have no arms to hold the hurting. They have no voice to speak the name of the voiceless. They have no tears to weep with the victim or power to push them forward.

Truth isn't compassion. Compassion isn't truth because it has no mind to judge between tree and human baby parts in an alley dumpster. It has no functional system able to produce lasting benefits for more. It has no determined insight to diagnose accurately and find the cure.

Truth is embodied. It is the epitome of good wrapped in human, according to the Bible's explanation. It's perfectly positioned to operate in an accurate assessment, productive system and on the flip side, in comfort, care, encouragement and inspiration to break free.

A genuine conversation, whether light or weighty, is marked by confidence and openness. Conversation is speaking and listening. If you are perfect, you only need to speak and not listen. If you are worthless you only need to listen and not speak.

Conversation, interacting truthfully, becomes an experience of death and rebirth. That's what listening, learning, trying out your thoughts by speaking, is.

> The popularity of the Joe Rogan Experience podcast or the Lex Fridman podcasts, for example, with millions tuning in, is what the supremacy of the logos sounds like.

Encountering truth brings transformation by nature.

It is no accident that truth ends up being a person in the scripture story. Let's never mind who for just a moment. Just that it is a person. That concept is worth thinking about for about twenty years, to start.

One of the most fundamental elements of Christianity, what is at the center of its structure and function, is the willingness to reform, update, go through the purifying fire, death, and rebirth.

What makes Jesus the truth, why He's labeled, "The Truth" in the Scripture narrative is, in part, because He is the one who gives Himself to judgment, death, and becomes the resurrection. He demonstrates, not just telling us, but acts out the definition of what truth is. He is that eternally in His role and relationship in the trinity and in the unfolding of God's plan in history.

41
The King

What is a king?

A king is where the state and the individual merge.

A king is the primary figure of the state, the primary representative of the individual citizen and therefore the primary mediation between the state and citizen.

A king is a ruler and leader.

A king rules by instituting law as well as providing sustenance and protection.

A king leads by making decisions on behalf of the nation as well as leading the fight against opposition and threat to the state.

Jesus is the fulfillment of the law and the one who defeats sin and death.

The Jewish people in the first century found themselves under the reign of the Roman Empire. They had their sites on a long-awaited Messiah to free them from Roman or any foreign rule. The problem was that true salvation couldn't be limited to the state level. The individual human heart was enslaved and needed to be set free.

Ironically, what the Jews did not see was that they had become enslaved by their own religious law and still had sin as a permanent enemy. They made the law and tradition king, and it was tyrannizing their hearts.

The sacrificial system should have been the indication for them that that law and tradition wasn't enough. There had to be an atonement rooted in God on their behalf.

When Jesus, the Logos, the Living Word, showed up and said that they were slaves to the law and tradition, it's not difficult to understand why they saw Him as a threat.

They were looking for state salvation. But you can't have state salvation that is true, good, and eternal that doesn't first have salvation at the individual level.

What was wrong with the law and tradition if God was the one who gave it to them?

They believed they had everything. They thought they had all the truth and complete truth. This isn't unique to early and first century Jews. This is a description of dogma and law as such. It's the totalitarian impulse. It's always a present risk.

If law, tradition, and dogma is king, then you will always be a slave. The cosmos, and God, are too vast and infinite to be limited to what you have, know, understand, and can do now.

With both law and the infinite, justice and mercy, truth and love being real all at the same time, it would only make sense that the mediating entity between each be the true king.

God is showing us through the narrative of the Old and New Testament, Law and Messiah, that what deserves to be held as the highest, is the entity that updates dogma and can fulfill the law or act it out. The King is the one who leads to freedom out from totalitarianism.

The king should be that which can both be true in all aspects and open to move forward. The one who can make things new and who can sacrifice for the future. The king should be that which dies and resurrects.

The King of kings should be the archetype of death and resurrection. Because reality, the cosmos and life, is composed of and functions by micro deaths and rebirths. This is true biologically, philosophically, psychologically, emotionally, and spiritually.

Jesus is the eternal transition from slave to free, confinement to liberation, past to future, deterioration to integration, and death to life.

Here is an exchange between Jesus and the Jewish leaders.

> So Jesus was saying to the Jews who had believed Him, "If you abide in My word [continually obeying My teachings and living in accordance

with them, then] you are truly My disciples. And you will know the truth [regarding salvation], and the truth will set you free [from the penalty of sin]." They answered Him, "We are Abraham's descendants and have never been enslaved to anyone. What do You mean by saying, 'You will be set free'?"

Jesus answered, "I assure you and most solemnly say to you, everyone who practices sin habitually is a slave of sin. Now the slave does not remain in a household forever; the son [of the master] does remain forever. So if the Son makes you free, then you are unquestionably free. I know that you are Abraham's descendants; yet you plan to kill Me, because My word has no place [to grow] in you [and it makes no change in your heart]. I tell the things that I have seen at My Father's side [in His very presence]; so you also do the things that you heard from your father."

Your father Abraham [greatly] rejoiced to see My day (My incarnation). He saw it and was delighted." Then the Jews said to Him, "You are not even fifty years old, and You [claim to] have seen Abraham?" Jesus replied, "I assure you and most solemnly say to you, before Abraham was born, I Am." So they picked up stones to throw at Him, but Jesus concealed Himself and left the temple."

—John 8:31–38; 56–59 (amp)

Jesus isn't King simply and only because He's stated as such by the Bible.

Just because you have the right answer for your math problem doesn't mean that you get a check mark for being correct. You have to "show your work." You have to demonstrate how you arrived at your answer, whether it's correct or not.

Jesus is the King because He's the Word. The Word is the Logos, which is the Truth that mediates between order and chaos, what is known and unknown.

He's the source of the concept of freedom of speech, the chief value. It's the basis for the meaning of freedom of the press. This is where the primacy of the logos would show up in a state.

He's the Word made flesh, wisdom, the master, the second Adam. He's the one who's reached the pinnacle following the fool, the amateur, the beginner, the first Adam.

He's the first. The first to keep God's Law. The first to satisfy the punishment for the human's crime. The first to overcome the temptation of evil by Satan. The first to resurrect to everlasting life.

There is a real link between the role and function of Christ and the philosophical essence of speech.

When John in his gospel opens with the Word being God the Creator, then becoming human, he's making the point that reason and communication is patterned after the second person of the trinity.

Logos is eternally central, the highest and supreme, because it is the element that mediates, connects and unites, ultimately in the trinity, between Father and Spirit.

The Word, the Logos is mediating between things in creation when; human is relating to human, when there is negotiation between the left and right brain hemispheres, when the value of free speech is at the pinnacle of rights for Western culture, when there's dialogue between differing opinions, when the will combines the mind and feelings to embody action.

Jesus is King because He holds all things together; between Father and Spirit in the Trinity, between God and creation, and between all things in the cosmos.

What Jesus is, and His position in the Trinity, eternally makes Him the one that functions in relation to the orderly law giving Father and the open infinite Spirit in a way that values both and holds both together.

He, then, is uniquely positioned to operate out towards God's creation, which was originally good and God glorifying. However, it got corrupted and separated from God, And Jesus is the one that brings God's creation back into union with Himself.

In a letter to a church in Colossae in the first century, Paul states and argues that Jesus "is the image of the invisible God; the first born, over all creation. Things in heaven and on earth, visible and invisible. Whether thrones or powers or rulers, or authorities, all things were created by Him and for Him. He's before all things and in Him, all things hold together. He is the head of the Body, the church. He is the beginning, and the first born from the dead. So that in everything, He might have the supremacy."

"There shall be no end to the increase of His government and of peace, [He shall rule] on the throne of David and over his kingdom, to establish it and uphold it with justice and righteousness from that time forward and forevermore."—Isaiah 9:7 (amp)

To be called a King of kings, you essentially have to possess all of the abstract characteristics and qualities across all kings everywhere from all time.

In Jesus' first coming, He isn't seen as a king ruling, but as a humble servant. Despite His lowly upbringing He becomes recognized as an ideal. He's held up as the highest, a human among humans.

A king functions both as an ideal, something to look up to, and a judge, a point of reference or standard. You cannot have an ideal without it simultaneously being judge. They go hand in hand. Jesus demonstrates this dichotomy in his first and second coming.

In His first coming He is presented as the highest, the ideal, the star in the sky for all to look up to and aim for. In His second coming He is seen as a Judge.

Why is Jesus seemingly emphasized as king and not the Father or Holy Spirit?

Perhaps because in part they are diametrically opposed and the one that sits between them has the role of ruling perfectly and righteously because he holds both in himself at the same time.

Let's keep in mind, in contrast to the description in the last paragraph, Jesus isn't stationary only, like holding a scale and keeping them in balance. It's far more sophisticated.

The nature of the trinity is the Father as law and order. The Holy Spirit is open and pioneer in relation to the infinite. God reveals himself in progression, in story. He unfolds Himself.

Jesus plays the central role eternally in the Godhead as well as in the redemption story.

The framework of the Trinity is the definition of what constitutes a story. There is a frame or state, then there is a movement away or an anomaly, and then there is a journey, and in humanity often through trial toward mending, growing, and learning.

Why would God choose to reveal himself through narrative?

God, revealing himself through narrative only makes sense if the nature of narrative is intricately tied to the fundamental nature of God Himself. The nature of the trinity matches the nature of narrative. The pattern of story as such, is coming from what the trinity is and how the triune God functions.

Now, because God as a trinity is eternal or always living, this pattern of structure, journeying out in the infinite, and then restructuring, becomes a cycle, an eternal cycle.

Everything falls into this narrative structure of order, chaos, and a journey navigating between them. It's constructed that way because it matches the basic nature of the triune God and the role and function of The Son.

It's not just that the story about God reveals God, it's that narrative as such reveals God. It reveals the Son. It reveals the son because narrative is shared, told, dramatized. The Son Jesus is the eternal Word, the full expression of God.

Jesus is King.

42
The Fool to Master: Part Two

"Or haven't you read in the law that on Sabbath days the priests in the temple violate the Sabbath and are innocent? I tell you that something greater than the temple is here.

The men of Nineveh will stand up at the judgment with this generation and condemn it, because they repented at Jonah's preaching; and look—something greater than Jonah is here. The queen of the south will rise up at the judgment with this generation and condemn it, because she came from the ends of the earth to hear the wisdom of Solomon; and look—something greater than Solomon is here."—Matt. 12:5–6; 41–42 (csb)

Earlier in the book we looked at the character and role of the Fool. The fool is the forerunner. He is the opener to the headliner. He is the first fruit.

Jesus arrives in the gospels as the Master in contrast to the characters and themes throughout the Old Testament.

All through His three-year ministry, people were addressing Jesus as, "Master." Fitting. An expert. One who walked and talked with authority.

Jesus was a master of the Law of Moses, a master of the Old Testament, a master of the Jewish tradition, a master in morality, a master in leadership and communication. He was a master over weather, water, plants, animals, demons. He was a master of mind, will and emotion. He was a master of the body. He was a master of prayer.

Jesus in the human experience and reality, mastered life. It's no accident that Jesus is, not only on, but at the top of the list of most influential and most admired humans in history. He is the greatest of all time.

In a message titled "Who Is This Jesus?" the late Timothy Keller, pastor of Redeemer Presbyterian Church, in Manhattan, New York, quotes G. K. Chesterton,

> "No one has ever yet discovered the word Jesus ought to have said or the deed He ought to have done. Nothing He does falls short. In fact, He is always surprising you and taking your breath away. Because He's better than you could imagine. Why? They are the surprises of perfection. He combined virtues never seen together. Tenderness without weakness. Strength without harshness. Humility without the slightest lack of confidence. Holiness and unbending convictions without the slightest lack of approachability. Power without insensitivity. Passion without prejudice. The harshest judgment on the self-satisfied, yet the most winsome kindness to the broken and the marginal. Never inconsistent. Never a false step. Never a jarring note."—Timothy Keller, "Who Is This Jesus? (Open Forum)", May 1, 1994. Copyright © Gospel in Life All Rights Reserved. https://gospelinlife.com/sermon/who-is-this-jesus-an-open-forum/

Jesus is the one where truth and love are present at the same time. The one where justice and mercy reside together. The one where condemnation and forgiveness are combined. Jesus is the finale, the one that the Old Testament stories were referring to, previewing, and leading toward.

I stated in the earlier chapter that the characters in the Bible play multiple roles at the same time. Here is something really cool. Jesus plays both roles of fool and wisdom.

He doesn't just contrast himself as Master, Savior to the characters of the O.T. and us as sinners. In contrast with Himself and His second coming, He identifies with us as fool, failure, the one who suffers, in His first coming. Then in His second coming he is the Lord and King.

In His first coming He tells two guys, "How foolish you are, and how slow to believe all that the prophets have spoken! Wasn't it necessary for the Messiah to suffer these things and enter into his glory?"—Luke 24:25–26 (csb)

In His first coming He identifies with us. "For we do not have a high priest who is unable to sympathize with our weaknesses, but one who has been tempted in every way as we are, yet without sin."—Hebrews 4:15 (csb)

When Satan was tempting Jesus in the desert, the temptation was to get Jesus to bypass the cross, to skip suffering. Jesus denied the temptation.

In His first coming, Jesus is crying out to the Father that if it's possible to let the cup of wrath and suffering pass by Him. Yet not His will, but His Fathers be done.

"He made the one who did not know sin to be sin for us, so that in him we might become the righteousness of God."—2 Corinthians 5:21 (csb)

In His first appearance he says, "Just as the Son of Man did not come to be served, but to serve, and to give his life as a ransom for many."—Matthew 20:28 (csb)

About His first coming, the writer of the book of Hebrews states, "But we do see Jesus— made lower than the angels for a short time so that by God's grace he might taste death for everyone . . . because he suffered death. For in bringing many sons and daughters to glory, it was entirely appropriate that God—for whom and through whom all things exist—should make the pioneer of their salvation perfect through sufferings."—Hebrews 2:9–10 (csb)

In Jesus' first coming He's riding on a donkey. In His second coming He's riding a stallion.

No wonder the Jewish scholars and leaders rejected Jesus. They were waiting for the conquering King, a Savior and Ruler. Not a lowly poor carpenter from some small town.

In His first coming Jesus identifies with evil, hate, crime, sinners, us, the failures, the fools. But in His second coming He is the Master, the King, the conquering Lord, the Judge. The Great Sovereign reigning over all.

How do we know that's who He will be in His second coming? How do we even know he is returning?

Because in one weekend He gave us both roles. He suffered and died on the cross, then three days later He walked out of a borrowed tomb in the middle east conquering sin and death. So, we can trust He will finish the story of history as the King.

Jesus is the transition from fool to wise, failure to success, slave to free, filth to clean, ill to health, death to life, guilty to righteous. Improvement of any sort, at any time, is meaningful and good because it points to, is reflective of its eternal source, God the Son, Jesus.

If your life is filled with micro improvements, but you have never met and subjected your life to the macro, the ultimate, the source of improvement, then all progress in your life is vain. It will run out, dry up, and die out.

What should you do? Take note of the pattern.

Identify with the one who is the eternal conversion and rebirth. You do this by confession, aligning with the reality of your true evil condition. Then agree that it deserves to be rightly judged, because right judgment is always good. Then ask Jesus, the eternal savior and king to convert you from death to life. He's the only one that can do it.

I was scrolling through social media the other day and came across a recent clip of Jim Carrey talking to an audience.

> I've had some challenges in the last couple of years myself, and ultimately I believe that suffering leads to salvation. We have to somehow accept and not deny but feel our suffering, and then we make one of two decisions. We either decide to go through the gate of resentment, which leads to vengeance, which leads to self-harm, which leads to harm to others. Or we go through the gate of forgiveness which leads to grace. Just as Christ did on the cross. He suffered terribly, and he was broken by it. To look on the people who were causing that suffering or the situation that was causing that suffering with compassion and with forgiveness, that's what opens the gates of heaven for all of us.—Mind Body Spirit, "Jim Carrey

on Jesus Christ", YouTube Video, 2:11. February 2, 2024. https://www.youtube.com/watch?v=xG7VhvBltOk

Jim Carrey's words, are true words and wise words.

43
The Judge Redeemer

I was flying into Puerto Rico, July 2017, with a team from my church. When I looked out the window, I could see hundreds of blue-tarped roofs. Months earlier Hurricane Maria had devastated the island. Our time there was spent doing roofing.

Storms judge. They judge the integrity of structure.

Water judges. When rain lands on a roof the water will find the cracks and holes. When there is a flood, infrastructure is tested.

There is a theme of water in and throughout the Bible narrative. You can say there is a theology of water.

In the opening storyline of the Bible there is a garden with water flowing through it, (Genesis 2:10).

In the concluding passages of the Bible, there is a river flowing in the Garden City, (Revelation 22:1–2).

Water plays a significant role throughout the Bible. It's in the opening lines of chapter one in Genesis. A few pages further, it takes center stage when It swallows and consumes all in the Noah story.

The story of the flood demonstrates much about the nature and element of water, including its magnitude and power. Its potential for destruction and consumption is put on full display.

Water is fluid and formless. It's chaos, potential, unknown, and the deep. It clues us into the reality of infinitude. If structure, borders, shores aren't built, kept, and maintained, then the threat of flooding is real and damning.

The absence of water, the desert, the wasteland, and drought, play a complementary role throughout the story.

Too much water, there's a flood. Not enough water, drought or desert.

Consume too much water, you drown. Drink no water, you die. Chaos tests structure.

> Therefore everyone who hears these words of mine and puts them into practice is like a wise man who built his house on the rock. The rain came down, the streams rose, and the winds blew and beat against that house; yet it did not fall, because it had its foundation on the rock. But everyone who hears these words of mine and does not put them into practice is like a foolish man who built his house on sand. The rain came down, the streams rose, and the winds blew and beat against that house, and it fell with a great crash.—Matthew 7:24–27 (niv)

When you step under the shower, the water is crashing against the body, and loosens the dirt from the skin. Water's nature functions by finding what is not united to the entire structure and carries it away.

Water functions in similar fashion inside the body when it is consumed.

In the Scripture narrative, water plays the role of chaos. It's the deep, the unknown.

Too much chaos or water will flood and drown. Not enough chaos or water will dehydrate, leading to too much structure and then corruption, filth and decay. But enough water, chaos, consumed every day is life-giving.

This is true in the physical element of water as a drink as well as psychologically and philosophically. It's ultimately true spiritually and theologically because it is rooted in the nature of the triune God. God is both personal and known as well as infinite and unknown.

Jesus walking into the consuming waters of John's baptism gives himself to the full weight and threat of the drowning waters, depicting the all-consuming reality that overpowers the human in death, and death on the cross. He walks out of the waters, following the Holy Spirit into the dry and dusty desert.

Jesus teaches and exclaims he is the well spring of water. "Everyone who drinks this water will be thirsty again, but whoever drinks the water I give them will never thirst. Indeed, the water I give them will become in them a spring of water welling up to eternal life.' The woman said to him, 'Sir, give me this water so that I won't get thirsty and have to keep coming here to draw water.' He told her, 'Go, call your husband, and come back.'"—John 4:13–16 (niv)

Jesus here, is communicating the reality that what the element of water is, is good and true because it is about and rooted in the nature of who and what He is. He then begins to demonstrate that very reality by washing over the woman by coming in contact with her person and getting into her business.

He moves to judge her, perfectly and rightly. He affirms what is good and what is worthy. At the same time moves to find the elements attached to her life that are corrupt, lacking, unworthy, and polluted. He then helps her see the need to be cleaned and separated from the dirt.

"On the last and most important day of the festival, Jesus stood up and cried out, 'If anyone is thirsty, let him come to me and drink. The one who believes in me, as the Scripture has said, will have streams of living water flow from deep within him.' He said this about the Spirit. Those who believed in Jesus were going to receive the Spirit."—John 7:37–39 (csb)

Jesus comes to the dry, bordered, stonewalled, up tight, orderly structure, and breaks through, bringing a stream of water through; allowing chaos, the deep, the unknown to have a rightful place to allow for renewal, cleansing, resting, and dreaming; like depicted in Psalm 23:2–3.

He faces the storming winds and waves crashing into and overtaking the boat and calms them.

He is the boat carrying Noah through the flooding waters.

He looks up from writing in the dirt on the ground, finds the cracks and the holes in the overbearing, orderly, male, privileged scribes and

Pharisees in their structured fortress, and lets the chaotic judging liquid spill in to show that they are out of sync with God Himself.

Without skipping a beat, He turns to the immoral, loose, anything goes, female and instructs her to tighten up, build walls that will be healthy and helpful to preserving and investing in her well-being and separate from the infinite sea of immorality. Nothing could be more affirming and beneficial than judging well. Jesus, the Living Water, does that, is that.

He doesn't have compassion for the woman to the neglect and justification of her sin. Love is compassionate as well as rooted in truth.

Hydrate. The general rule is to drink eight glasses of water every day. Enough chaos to keep you fresh, tested, on your toes, and engaged. Too much could drown you, not enough will dehydrate you.

Jesus is perfectly positioned between the Father and the Spirit. He is the answer. He's positionally and functionally the answer.

You may have found eternal foundational bedrock to stand on. But if its limited to the drawn lines between your personality, political wing, economic status, religious denomination, theology, or education, against what is also eternally foundational bedrock, then you are in grave danger of only possessing ideology, partial reality. It's a limited and damning stance.

The triune God is eternally valuing, depending on, functioning with each of its persons in perfect unity and harmony, always. And it is the Son who judges perfectly to see where you stand.

Jesus is depicted in the Bible as the Judge and the Word. Those two elements go together. Words judge by nature.

> A man's stomach will be satisfied with the fruit of his mouth; He will be satisfied with the consequence of his words. Death and life are in the power of the tongue, and those who love it and indulge it will eat its fruit and bear the consequences of their words.—Proverbs 18:20–21(amp)
>
> All Scripture is God-breathed [given by divine inspiration] and is profitable for instruction, for conviction [of sin], for correction [of error

and restoration to obedience], for training in righteousness [learning to live in conformity to God's will, both publicly and privately—behaving honorably with personal integrity and moral courage]; so that the man of God may be complete and proficient, outfitted and thoroughly equipped for every good work.—2 Timothy 3:16–17 (amp)

For the word of God is living and active and full of power [making it operative, energizing, and effective]. It is sharper than any two-edged sword, penetrating as far as the division of the soul and spirit [the completeness of a person], and of both joints and marrow [the deepest parts of our nature], exposing and judging the very thoughts and intentions of the heart. And not a creature exists that is concealed from His sight, but all things are open and exposed, and revealed to the eyes of Him with whom we have to give account.—Hebrews 4:12–13 (amp)

In the beginning [before all time] was the Word (Christ), and the Word was with God, and the Word was God Himself.

In Him was life [and the power to bestow life] . . .

And the Word (Christ) became flesh, and lived among us; and we [actually] saw His glory, glory as belongs to the [One and] only begotten Son of the Father, [the Son who is truly unique, the only One of His kind, who is] full of grace and truth (absolutely free of deception).

For the Law was given through Moses, but grace [unearned, undeserved favor of God] and truth came through Jesus Christ. No one has seen God [His essence, His divine nature] at any time; the [One and] only begotten God [that is, the unique Son] who is in the intimate presence of the Father, He has explained Him [and interpreted and revealed the awesome wonder of the Father].—John 1:1–2; 14; 17–18 (amp)

And I saw heaven opened, and behold, a white horse, and He who was riding it is called Faithful and True (trustworthy, loyal, incorruptible, steady), and in righteousness He judges and wages war [on the rebellious nations]. His eyes are a flame of fire, and on His head are many royal crowns; and He has the name inscribed [on Him] which no one knows or understands except Himself. He is dressed in a robe dipped in blood, and His name is called The Word of God. And the armies of heaven, dressed in fine linen, [dazzling] white and clean, followed Him on white horses. From His mouth comes a sharp sword [His word] with which He may strike down the nations, and He will rule them with a rod of iron; and He will tread the wine press of the fierce wrath of God, the Almighty [in judgment of the rebellious world]. And on His robe and on His thigh He has a name inscribed, "KING OF KINGS, AND LORD OF LORDS."—Revelation 19:11–16 (amp)

The Word of God, the Living Word, the Logos, are not just arbitrary communicative references of the reality of writing, language and speech, but where these human elements find their origin, function and meaning in the first place.

Critical thought, thinking about thinking, being articulate, specifying your speech is judgment by nature. It dispenses with just about all possible thoughts and words, then selects a few to speak to make clear and concise. It brings to light what is accurate, right, and good. This is the function of Jesus, the second person of the trinity, as the Logos, the Living Word.

Words, speech, and communication mediate between two or more entities. It brings information to instruct, enlighten, inform, or correct. Jesus operates in this precise way. He is the Living Water, the Living Word, the Judge and Redeemer.

44
The Door

I pulled into my parking spot on a side street intersection across from my home in a northwest side neighborhood of Chicago. It would be equivalent to something like the Bronx, in New York. It was about 9:30 at night. It was dark, but there was still plenty of illumination from the streetlights.

Just before I opened my door to get out, I saw in between two parked cars across the street, what looked like a decent sized dog trotting down the sidewalk. But something in me told me that it wasn't a dog.

I took a look at the tail. Sure enough, that tail was pretty large and furry. This was no dog. It was a coyote! I couldn't believe it.

After it pranced by, I lost sight of it. Knowing that I had to get to my house, which was in the same direction the coyote headed, I sat waiting in the car for a few minutes. Then I decided to make my way home.

I stepped out of my car, gently closed the car door, and began my way across the street, eyes straining and looking in all directions. Once I crossed the intersection and reached the sidewalk of the side of the street my house was on, I looked, and there, about halfway down the block, sitting in the middle of the sidewalk, was the coyote.

My house was only the second house from the corner. But after a moment of seeing the coyote, I was trying to figure out in which direction it was looking.

I began to make my way toward the side gate, which led down the gangway toward the back of my house where the entrance was. The gate was about fifteen feet from the main sidewalk. Before I turned and headed toward the gate, I took one last glance toward the coyote.

At that moment I saw it get up and start to move quickly down the sidewalk. Before I had time to figure out which direction it was heading, I turned and began rushing toward the gate, holding my keys in hand ready to unlock it.

As I put the key to the lock, it wouldn't insert into the lock. I tried again and still it wouldn't insert. It was the wrong key! I fumbled the keys in my hand to get the right key. As I did, they slipped out of my hand and fell to the ground!

At that moment I knew I had a choice. Do I turn around and check to see if the coyote is near, or do I focus to get the right key in hand? If I turned to look for the coyote it would slow me down from getting the key.

I stooped down, grabbed my keys, got the right key, put it into the lock and unlocked the gate. As it swung open, I swiftly stepped inside, closed the gate, and locked it behind me. City slicker, now safe from the wild beast.

Gates are mentioned quite often in the Bible storyline. They are mentioned and stated almost as if they have some significance beyond a prop or dramatic detail to help bring a story to life.

"Give us the gate key."

"I have no gate key."

"Fezzik, tear his arms off."

"Oh, you mean this gate key."—Reiner, Rob, director. *The Princess Bride*. USA: 20th Century Studios, Metro-Goldwyn-Mayer, Lionsgate, Vestron Pictures, 1987, Film.

Throughout ancient history, cities were constructed with walls. They had city gates that would allow for passage in and out of the city. The walls were there for protection against all outside and unknown threats such as wild animals, enemies, and foreigners. The gate to the city functioned as a filter, a screen, a practical means of deciding what was allowed in and out.

This concept is rooted in the nature of how we function at all levels of reality.

Our home has doors and windows, all for the sole purpose of what and who is allowed passage in and out. Many homes and properties around the globe have walls and gates around the home.

The body has skin that functions as a border, with several passageways in and out of the body allowing for the function of the will on what is allowed in and out.

A wall or border plays a few different beneficial roles. It provides protection. It provides identity by distinction and unity. It provides stability, allowing for constant beneficial flow in and out.

The gate, the door, allows for resources that benefit what's inside to be allowed in: provisions, guests, information. It also allows for things that are inside to travel outside: exploration, growth, development, even waste.

Borders with no gates or doors, no passageway in or out, are too restrictive and are not fit for living.

In ancient warfare, armies would surround a city and not allow for any passage in or out. Essentially the city would run out of its resources and need to surrender or become so weak and vulnerable as a result that they would be overtaken by their enemy.

Should the goal be to remove all borders, walls, and boundaries so that exploration, growth or new experience can be maximized? Probably not. In part because there is a shadow, a downside to the outside, the unknown, the infinite.

Should the goal be to construct walls, borders, and boundaries so high and thick, with no gates, no doors, no windows or passageways in or out, to maximize preservation of what is and eliminate all outside threat? Probably not. In part because it doesn't take into account that there is a threat just as dangerous on the inside that needs to be addressed.

The goal is to build as a part of the wall or border, a gate or door that is strong; able to withstand the fiercest attack from a natural storm, wild animal, or enemy. But it should be able to function with relative ease to allow for regular and constant passage in and out.

There needs to be a way to benefit from maintaining what is of value on the inside as well as the pursuit of what is of value on the outside. At the same time a means of ridding what is of less value on the inside and fighting off what is of less value on the outside.

The prosperity, the well-being of living depends on it for a city, a nation, a home, a place of business, a website, a body, a mind, a relationship, a being.

The cosmos, our world, our humanity, functions with the reality of borders. We can hardly imagine it being any other way.

There is no definition of any particular one thing without border or boundary. We see and make sense of reality by what is distinct from all else. If it wasn't that way, then all would be one, and we could not function or be.

If there was only border and boundary and distinction without connection or meaning of relationship between any one thing to another, then we would be stuck, no reason to move, no understanding of how to see or function.

The passageway, the gate or door, stands, stating that the value of the border, what it holds inside and protects from outside is of ultimate importance. At the same time, it swings open, demonstrating, dramatizing, exclaiming that what is outside, what's beyond, what's different, what's new, that there is more, is of greatest importance.

Consider these words from Jesus:

> I am the gate. If anyone enters by me, he will be saved and will come in and go out and find pasture.—John 10:9 (csb)

> I and the Father are one.—John 10:30 (csb)

> I am the way, the truth, and the life. No one comes to the Father except through me. —John 14:6 (csb)

Jesus sits between the structured Father and the open Spirit, eternally mediating, opening and closing.

It doesn't seem to be a coincidence that God instructed the Israelites, enslaved in Egypt in the Exodus, the going out story, to take blood and put it on the doorway of their homes. It signifies that the means by which judgment and life are obtained is through sacrifice.

Of course, we are familiar with the imagery of the sacrificial lamb and the blood being a preview to Jesus on the cross. But it is placed on the doorway, the passageway from in and out, from home and the known to the forever infinite. I don't think that was arbitrary.

The second person of the Trinity, Jesus, the Son, is the door.

45
Communication

> I'm thrilled the white house called me tonight, because I'm actually working on a hip-hop album. It's a concept album about the life of someone I think embodies hip-hop, Treasury Secretary Alexander Hamilton. You laugh, but it's true. He was born a penniless orphan in Saint Croix, of illegitimate birth. He became George Washington's right-hand man. Became Treasury Secretary. Caught beef with every other Founding Father, and all on the strength of his writing. I think he embodies the words ability to make a difference.—The Obama White House, "Lin-Manuel Miranda Performs at the White House Poetry Jam: (8 of 8)", YouTube Video, 4:26. November 2, 2009. https://youtu.be/WNFf7nMIGnE

What is communication?

Communication is formulated expression.

In order to have communication there has to be an informed or structured entity. The structure then forms particular thoughts and pushes them out to share with another. Communication includes the use of speech, language, words, text, air, sound, and gestures.

The Bible narrative states that Jesus, the second person in the Trinity is the Word. I believe this analogy gives us direct insight into the essence of Jesus and His eternal function and role.

Speech that is organized, aligned, and reflecting the eternal structure in God the Father is a perfect representation of God.

Communication reveals, mediates, and transforms by its fundamental nature.

1. Communication is revelatory

Communication is thoughts that come out of a person. Communication gets pushed out by a defined living entity. Because the words come directly from within that entity, they express something true and accurate about what that entity is. The speech and words reveal something about the entity because the entity decided to share and express.

This happens through the union of outward air flow, sound from the vocal cords, and language all traveling outward from the will of the particular being. The speech comes out. Once hidden within, now out and able to be heard, or seen. It's revealed.

What is revealed is decided by the being, but the fundamental reality is that speech reveals by nature. It's a window, a door from which something from the inside comes out. In turn, allows for anyone outside to see inward.

Jesus eternally functions as the second person in the Trinity by coming from the unified Father and Spirit God and revealing Him. "He is the image of the invisible God."—Colossians 1:15 (csb)

Speech can be used to define or express accurately. Or it can be used to explore and experiment, like when we say, "I'm just thinking out loud."

Orderly types use their speech to define. Open types use their speech to express and explore.

Conservatives use speech to diagnose. They want the facts. They use reason and logic. Liberals use speech to create, bring awareness, and survey.

Both are vital and right uses of speech.

This general description seems to be a fundamental distinction between man and woman, conservative and liberal, orderly personality and open personality, the reformed or fundamentalist evangelical and the charismatic or progressive evangelical. The list is endless.

If language is only used to articulate facts, it fails to communicate and reveal all that is, since there are aspects of reality that are less known and understood, and certainly that which is unknown altogether. Such as the deep psyche and experience of the human being, and the complexities of the universe.

Language is certainly capable of revealing what is understood. But what of beauty, mystery and the infinite?

In enters the artists, the lyricists, the vocalists, the rappers, the poets, the novelists, the comedians, masters of words. Referencing what we know but leading into the darkness or blinding light of what we know nothing about.

2. Communication is mediation

Communication is nonexistent if there is nothing or if there is just a one-dimensional singularity and nothing else.

In order for communication to be a thing, there has to be multiple elements because communication functions necessarily as a reality operating between two or more entities.

The term communication has its roots in the unity between things.

The meaningfulness of communication rests on the fact that it connects things. It's between things. We can share and express through language because others are there to hear, receive and interact with what is articulated.

Communication bonds.

It's the Son that gets sent from heaven to earth. The Son is the mediator between God and man.

However, He doesn't take this on as a new role once history needs it. He is fit to function and meet history's needs because he functions in the role eternally. Mediation is His fundamental nature as the second person of the Trinity, mediating between the Father and Spirit.

Because communication mediates, it brings separate entities together; opening to allow another to see and know oneself, as well as learn and receive another through the transfer of information. Jesus does this eternally between the Father and the Spirit as well as between God and human.

"The Word became flesh and dwelt among us. We observed his glory, glory as the one and only Son from the Father, full of grace and truth . . . No one has ever seen God. the one and only Son, who is himself God and is at the Father's side—he has revealed him."—John 1:14, 18 (csb)

3. Communication is transformative

How does the finite and infinite coexist?

Knowledge is infinite, we are finite. In order to continue to be able to contend and function in the reality of the infinite, we have to continue to update, transform, and be informed.

Communication functions as a transformative reality by nature.

Tyranny or force can produce particular action from a person or persons. But the action will not be believed in or held to in and throughout the entire person. There is fragmentation, which means the action cannot be sustained.

Deception and/or misinformation can produce particular action, but it ultimately produces fragmentation and severance from outside reality, which will lead to failure.

Optimistic wishing can move the emotions and inspire for a moment, but without being grounded and connected to what is true, it will fizzle and fade.

Truthful explanation is able to reach the mind, go all the way down into the soul, sift and test thought and belief, produce a change in mind, heart, will, and action and be sustained.

Not only does truth bring the individual person into alignment with themselves but brings the person into alignment with all reality for all time.

Communication provides new information, allowing for adjustment and updating. It throws out old info, bad info, and incorporates the new. This reality will never be exhausted or secondary. In order to be living and ever living, communication is a central element.

In the opening lines of the Bible, the narrative goes from "formless and void ... darkness was upon the face of the deep." to "saw that it was good," through the means of "God said."—Genesis 1 (amp)

When you learn something new, something old dies, gets left behind, burned away, and you are changed to incorporate what is new. This reality and its function find its origin in the second person of the trinity as the one who acts this out in history in the crucifixion and resurrection, the epitome of death and rebirth.

These two realities, Jesus' death and resurrection and the function of communication as a transformative activity, aren't loosely connected or have happenstance relation. They are the same operation being demonstrated at different levels of analysis.

Words, or communication, put in form. they transform. If it is true communication, and it is received, that which receives it will be put in a form that will last. They will be informed.

Because Jesus is the true revealing expression of God, the purest truest reality, if He is believed, then we can be transformed, reformed, put in form and in alignment with that which is eternally good and functional.

Jesus is the Word, the communication, the Logos that reveals God to us.

He mediates between God and humans.

He shows us where we are wrong, what we are missing as ones disconnected from the ever-living God and gives us what we need, by informing us.

This role then of communication has these primary functions wherever it shows up in our human experience because it finds its origination in the eternal God described in the Bible.

So, if anything has a hope of being healthy and functioning, the need for communication, the freedom to reveal, to mediate and to transform will always need to be present.

It has this primary role in a just society in the freedom of speech and freedom of the press.

It has this primary role in any functional intimate relationship, friendship, or partnership.

When John opens his gospel by stating that Jesus is the Word, He's saying that communication as such is a type of Christ.

Let's look at three means of communication.

Dialogue

Are there any two people ever, who have agreed on everything? I don't think so.

The necessity for dialogue in order to not only relate but remain functional and progress is essential.

We are finite in the face of the infinite. Infinite potential and infinite threat. In the face of ignorance, lack of motivation, or trouble, dialogue can transfer useful and encouraging information.

Others know, but I don't, and I can learn what I need to through dialogue. I know what others don't and can benefit them through dialogue.

Debate, arguing, or discussion then, becomes a human fundamental.

We are all worthy of shared information because we are God's creatures.

Dialogue can be a primary pathway forward.

This is true in all intimate relationships.

Perhaps this is the reason why God has Prayer and reading His Word as fundamental spiritual disciplines.

In order to dialogue, you have to be able to articulate accurately, express honestly, listen openly, and process carefully.

If healthy dialogue isn't at the heart of your relationships, whatever their nature, then the relationships will fragment and die.

Confession

There is something about confessing that brings healing. The alignment between your thoughts, action, and speech makes you stronger. Why wouldn't it?

Confessing convicts. It indicts. It's stating something that is wrong about you. This becomes an acknowledgement and agreement with the judgment on you.

Confession brings an alignment of a person with true reality, which is a relief and liberating.

It is also an alignment with guilt and shame, which hurts and is troubling.

So, there's a paradox here. One that is central to God's means of redemption and salvation.

When we confess our wrong, we align our speech with God and what is ultimately good and right, against what is faulty and deserving to be dispensed with. This brings us into judgment. But if we do it voluntarily, we also side with the reality that is good, right and worthy of continuing.

Jesus, the one who is silent under accusation and receives God's judgment on the cross for sinners, and walks out of the tomb in resurrection, is the one that our confession is ultimately in subjection to, or what confession is patterned after.

This is because Jesus is acting out the function of confession when He goes to the cross, dies, is buried and resurrects.

Confession then is right and good because it's the means by which we are united and brought into alignment with Him.

Writing

I've heard from different psychologists that writing can be a means of healing. Like confession, there is something about facing something in your life by writing it out, letting it out, and trying to articulate it that produces mending.

By writing, you are facing the trouble head on. You are taking what is inside and expressing it. You are also processing it, which allows you to sift through it and judge it.

Text becomes just another form of communication with all of its functions.

There is an insistence on the centrality of God's written word in the Bible. Because the Bible is communication, spoken or written from the place where communication and text find their origin, namely God, it makes the Bible the supreme authority, necessarily.

46
Psychology

Psychology as a practice, has utility because communication works as a transforming reality.

A psychologist is a trained professional in the arena of the inner being, personality, and life's circumstances. They don't know everything, and they don't know the particulars of any given client's life, so they have to listen and talk.

The person meeting with a psychologist is out of form in one or more ways. They need to be put in form or gain information. They don't know everything, and so in order to gain understanding, they have to talk, try, and articulate or accurately assess where they are, what's wrong, and what they need to do.

If we know everything or know what we think we should, but aren't what we desire or should be, then our knowledge hasn't become integrated with all that we are.

If we don't know what we ought, then we have to open up and be willing to both put to death things that are wrong, old, or hindering, and allow for something new to take root and bear fruit.

Oftentimes this begins with what we think.

Transformation happens by the renewal of the mind (see Romans 12:2).

Communication allows for the transfer of information to be received and incorporated in thought and essentially in lifestyle. if it's accurate and true, no matter how difficult it is to share or hear, it has the power to be received and incorporated; pushing old broken beliefs out and allowing for strong durable reality to reside and become a part of your structured being.

Psychology should help you face reality as honestly as possible. It should help set an upward aim and make decisions to step toward that aim. This is made possible by the means of communication.

Communication in psychology helps face and express reality honestly. It allows you to sort, sift and decide on a particular path toward improvement.

Jesus functions in this way as the one who reveals God perfectly and our condition perfectly. He is the judge between what is good and bad; what is godlike and what is immoral.

We see why he would function as a judge of us as God's image bearers who decided to go our own way. He images the perfect ideal and reaches us as the one sent out and down to us. He is able to test what matches His true perfect likeness to God and what doesn't.

Jesus doesn't just function as a judge who condemns all, but as a means to be transformed and brought back to God (see John 3:17).

When the earth is formless and void, darkness over the very great deep, it's God's spoken word that flows out and forms and shapes it.

Communication, words, text, tell us something fundamental about the nature of God. God in the second person of the Trinity, Jesus, demonstrates something fundamental about the nature of communication.

Psychology works to the degree it functions in likeness to the reality of the God defined in the Bible. In particular, the second person of the Trinity who reveals honestly, mediates lovingly, and transforms beneficially.

47

Education

Critical Thinking

Education is learning information about or training in a particular field or subject.

We live in the domain of the known and unknown. Education formalizes the process of moving us from unknown to known.

There is a fundamental value in the human experience of not being stuck or ignorant. It's not just knowing that is of value, but the process by which we gain knowledge. Education becomes key, then.

Growth and development are central to the human as a living being. We see this in the value of education.

Education is a process by nature.

You are sitting in your first day of high school history class. Your teacher tells the class that he will lecture for three weeks and then give a test. You look over to the corner of the classroom. There sits a filing cabinet, or perhaps, a computer on the teacher's desk with a folder in it. Inside the hard copy folder or e-folder is the answer key to all of the tests for the class.

Now, you are going to sit in that class for an hour every day for weeks, listening and discussing, just to get to the answers that are sitting right there in the classroom already.

If the teacher wants you to have the answers, and they have the answers, why all of that time spent teaching and listening; when they can just open up that file, hand you/email you a copy, and call it a day?

You are in your high school algebra class. You still remember your teacher's name, and the kids who had no problems with algebra who aced every test; that wasn't me. You turn in your homework with all of your answers circled. Your teacher follows up with you and says, "you got the right answer for number six, but you didn't show your work."

What's your response? "And?"

Having the correct answer isn't the highest value. It's knowing how to produce or reach the right answer. Because mathematics is such a large field and it's virtually impossible to memorize all the correct answers to all equations, it's important to know the process of reaching the correct answer.

The element of studying, rehearsing, memorizing, learning, is central to a good education, perhaps more so than being given correct answers. Learning how to contend, think, analyze, engage with new information is a value that serves the "finite, made for the infinite" human for all time in all circumstances.

A few years back after daydreaming about what it would be like to win the lottery, I began to move past the pleasant thoughts about material purchases, traveling, and charity and tried to imagine what it would really be like to have that much money.

I quickly realized that there would be some significant guard rails and parameters removed that would open up some temptations that could possibly lead me to bad places.

It's not obvious that I would be better off having so much money. It's quite possible if not probable that my character couldn't handle the access to that degree of excess.

In a similar fashion, we are living in the information age. If you want to know it, you have access to it.

Is this good?

It could be good, but with the excess of information, it's not obvious that we are able to process the amount of information we have access to.

The process of examining, being critical, judging, is the means of deciding what is worthy of holding and incorporating.

Jesus functions as the means and process by which we move from death to life, blind to sight, broken to mended, dirty to clean, hell bound to heaven bound.

Education works and is useful because its fundamental nature is rooted in the nature of the second person of the trinity. Jesus is the willing sufferer, the judge who tests and filters. He's the process, the pathway.

Broad is the way that leads to destruction, but narrow is the way that leads to eternal life.—Matthew 7:13-14. That's not religious, that's a genius proverb for all humans for all time, in all circumstances.

Education is a function patterned after Christ, by nature.

Conclusion

Jesus is:
The Ideal
The Will
The Mediation
The Revealer
The Transformer
The Passage
The Training
The Conditioning
The exercising
The Work Out
The Apprenticeship
The Filter
The Screen
The Integration
The Assimilation

When God creates, He reproduces Himself out in a myriad of ways. When the creation becomes corrupted, the Son goes out to redeem. The creation is worthy of redemption because it's about God and for God in the first place.

Jesus is the singularity, the prototype. God and the cosmos are wrapped up in Him.

The framework of Chaos and Order along with the mediating reality between them that make up the cosmos and our existence, finds its origination in the nature of the three persons of the trinity.

If this is true, if the nature of God is the pattern used to create, and Christ is the central figure, then everything, including the psychological, philosophical, political, personal, biological, and phenomenological becomes, is, a type of Christ. Not loosely or arbitrarily, of course. Quite the contrary. With great intention and sophistication.

Perhaps not Christ only, but the Holy Spirit and God the Father as well, given the analogies included throughout the book.

So, when God creates and calls it good, the cosmos is God, or Christ, abstracted out in a multiplicity of ways. Yes, the creation is separate from God, is not God, but it is coming from Him as well as reflecting him in the very nature of its design, (*see* Romans 11:33–36).

Each part then, is actively and quite literally displaying the glory of Christ in its particular design, position and function.

Any corruption of God's creation then, becomes counter God and anti-Christ necessarily.

Everything as a type of Christ . . . that can't be right. Everything as a type of Christ, type of Holy Spirit and type of God the Father, that's . . . too much.

If it were true, for starters it would require artists, composers, producers, musicians, writers, painters, sculptors, dancers, actors, interior designers, fashion designers, chefs, scientists, biologists, astrophysicists, psychologists, tradesman, engineers, architects, plumbers, construction workers, landscapers, welders, sociologists, businessmen, attorneys, philosophers, researchers, historians, theologians, educators, athletes, comedians, politicians, and so on, all working together for about an eternity just to begin to see it and glorify God in it, through it and for it.

Why didn't God just only form a large stone with a mouth and maybe two arms raised, that sits before His throne for eternity that proclaims, "holy, holy holy" constantly? Because even then we would have to ask why any form rather than no form? Why a mouth? Why "holy"? Why raised arms?

Even in the Bible we see the flowering of complexity with its varying genres, multiple authors, written in different parts of the world, over the course of several centuries.

The depth, layering, multiplicity, and diversity in the cosmos along with earthly human experience, down to its finest detailed fragments, is showing us God.

What precisely is the cosmos, history, life and its meaning, if it is not a microcosm and composition of microcosms of God.

When I listen to professionals speak from their particular field of expertise, I hear them describing the nature of their field, as well as the nature of God.

We prioritize God over and above all things not simply because of their difference from God, but also because of their relation to and commonality with God of whom He is their origin and eternal blueprint.

THE SHADOW: A POT SHOT
Don't put all your eggs in one basket.

48
An Introduction

Fredrick Nietzsche, German philosopher, and critic of Christian religion, in the second half of the nineteenth century, proclaimed the death of God. Jordan Peterson says that Nietzsche prophesied that as a result of God's death, it wouldn't be possible to wash away all of the blood from the ideas, concepts, and worldviews that would rush in to take His foundational place. The twentieth century has proved this horror correct.

With God as the highest ideal and source of all good, the one in perfect balance between order and chaos, removed from the picture, we fall prey to two extremes.

There's nihilism on one side; everything is meaningless. The relative, post-modern, deconstructive, open, infinite abyss swallows up the meaning of any particularity.

On the other side is totalitarianism. Everything is contained in what I see, know, understand, and desire. It contaminates the inside and makes all others, enemies.

With totalitarianism, the downfall is becoming too conservative, orderly, hierarchal, or tyrannical. On the left you fall prey to compassion, equity, self-identification, and universalism.

The extremes are polar opposites. They are diametrically opposed. So, when they are in balance, each valuing the other without losing distinction, there is harmony. This is where and when life is present, always.

When there is a pull too hard in one direction, overcompensation, severance or disconnect between the two, the shadow emerges.

The shadow is necessarily linked to each value. The highest value and aim then, is union. Union in relation to who and what God is as a triune being, and defined as we have defined Him, becomes a technical central value.

In this order/chaos framework is culture and nature. Both are necessary for life.

Culture, in relation to nature, is masculine; orderly, and structured. It is the benevolent Father. However, it has a shadow. If not kept in check, it turns into tyranny.

Nature is feminine; open, mysterious, and life giving. It's the benevolent mother. But it has a shadow. If not kept in check, it will devour with storms, illness, and catastrophe.

If you only relate to culture as the benevolent father and are blind to its shadow, you will be susceptible to tyranny, corruption, harsh judgment, sterilization, and slavery.

If you only relate to nature as the benevolent mother and are naïve to its shadow, you will be susceptible to over-protecting, coddling and flooding.

If you listen to the current radicals on the Left in the west, they accuse the right of being a racist oppressive patriarchy that only benefits the majority and those at the top.

The left, the person who is open and liberal, is afraid of solitary confinement. The right, the person who is orderly and conservative, is afraid of chaotic anarchy.

As a part of the introductory passages in the Bible, we find two stories, told back-to-back.

The first is how the earth began to be populated and filled with people. However, they grew in their immorality, sin, and distance from their reflection of God. God responds to this by sending a flood to kill all living creatures.

There seems to be a description of no rules, anything goes, whatever is in the heart, mind, and wish of the human to do. God's response is a flood, as if giving them over to their desires.

When there is no order, the flood waters consume.

The second story almost seems like a response to the catastrophe of the flood.

The people are unified in language and decide to build a high tower. God's response to the structure and unity around erecting it is upsetting their high aim by giving them different languages. this brings disunity, the failure to build the tower, and the dispersion of the people.

What is God's deal?

The people in the first story are doing what God told them to do, "Be fruitful, multiply."—Genesis 1:28 (csb)

In the second story people are doing what God wants them to do, be united and aim upward.

The problem for each is that they seek and pursue one of the fundamental values without and in opposition to the other. Immorality brings the flood. Idolatry brings division.

In both scenarios, God provides the remedy.

In the flood, He provides the unifying word that provides a structure able to move through the flood waters and come out safely on the other side. In the story of the tower, He sends a dividing word, so they don't get stuck on a unified mission toward hell.

Both stories move the entire Bible narrative toward the arrival and work of the actual Messiah. He is the Living Word who holds all things together, and rightly divides, which leads to everlasting life.

It's the union in and of God that makes Him a personal-infinite, and essentially living God.

God is three persons. Each person is uniquely and fully God. There is only one God. This is what is described in the Bible.

Even throughout church history there has been a swing from one side to the other, on this triune description.

It has been defined as three different God's, each separate, and not one. On the other side, it has been defined as one God with no separate, distinct persons who are each God.

There is a unifying emphasis to the point that is wrong, and there is a multiplicity emphasis to the point that is wrong. Surprise, surprise.

What it may mean that each person of the trinity is fully God is each is in perfect harmony with the attributes of the others within Himself. For example, while the Father's primary nature has the fatherly characteristics, within himself He also has characteristics that particularly define the other two persons.

There is perfect harmony and unity in God. God being in perfect relation to His creation is right in line with who He is eternally.

So, when we decided to break from the ultimate eternal reality, the triune God who is in perfect harmony, we brought a division into our own being and all of creation.

That division leaves us violently thrashing back and forth between order and chaos without a stabilizing relationship between the two. If we aren't thrashing back and forth, we are pressing with all of our being toward one of them, clinging to it as a savior and denouncing and cursing the other.

This leads to death. It is death. It is the fundamental problem at every level of analysis of life and reality. It all stems from being separated from a God who is triune.

Don't overplay your hand. Don't overplay your hand. Do not overplay your hand.

Each person of the Trinity and the pattern in the cosmos that comes from the Trinity, when cut off and separated from the others, brings a shadow directly tied to one of the persons.

Jordan Peterson describes the evil triad of, "arrogance, resentment, and deceit."—Abel, "Of Course Mom. 'Arrogance, Resentment, and Deceit are the Evil Triad' – Jordan B. Peterson", YouTube Video, 1:05, April 22, 2023.

https://www.youtube.com/watch?v=_IWcBOxEJmY

Each of those is tied to the particular description we have been discussing in this book. Let's take a moment and look at these shadows.

49
Arrogance and Tyranny

What precisely is the difference between order and slavery? The pursuit of a goal and tightening the borders to the point where you have concluded that you have reached the top, have everything you need, and know enough, is never completely true. Acting like it, leads to division and death.

> One of the things people have often said about Germany was that it was a very civilized country and yet it descended into barbarity. But conscientiousness is a very good predictor of long-term success. And so, you can say, conscientious societies are more "civilized", but they're also more orderly. And that makes them more disgust sensitive. So, what have might easily been in Germany, was that it was an excess of civilization, rather than its lack, that produced these consequences. And that's a far more frightening proposition, and one that's, I believe, much more likely to be true.—Jordan Peterson Fan Channel, "Why Hitler Bathed Even More Than You Think—Prof. Jordan Peterson", YouTube Video, 5:49, September 12, 2017. https://youtu.be/XBu6xI1iUM0

What a brilliant observation. It was the fact of too much order, and the repulsion of being open that led to the horrors of Auschwitz.

The vast majority of reaction is blind reaction, operating under the guise of thoughtfulness and righteous critique. But it ultimately proves detrimental because it's only critical in one direction.

Think about what it means to build a strong immune system. You can't do it by sterilizing. You do it by constantly and deliberately exposing yourself to risk.

Jonathan Haidt, a social psychologist in an interview on "The 'Stunning Fragility' and Vindictive Political Correctness of Today's Students," states,

I think the best analogy here is to understand what's happening with peanut allergies. Why are peanut allergies rising? They've been rising at an alarming rate since the 90's. And so, what do we do? I take my kids to school; we get these long lectures on how we can't have any peanut butter in school. . . . a report came out last year, do you know why peanut allergies are rising? Because we haven't exposed kids to peanuts. That's the reason they're rising.—Gravitahn, "The 'Stunning Fragility' & Vindictive Political Correctness of Today's Students—Jonathan Haidt", YouTube Video, 13:36, April 4, 2017. https://youtube/snqXOvnHzcQ

There are reasons for things like order, borders, and disinfectants. But if you try to cram all that is good into that domain, you will end up in totalitarianism. It will be an ideology that does not match that which is eternally true and good, namely the God that is triune in nature.

Fundamentalists, totalitarians, and the proud all fall prey to the shadow of orderliness and holiness.

Friedrich Nietzsche stated, "Convictions are more dangerous enemies of truth than lies."—Friedrich Nietzsche, *Human, All Too Human* (1878), 264.

Drawing hard and fast lines can be as much of a danger as an indication of being right. You better double check and keep on checking where you have drawn your moral lines.

Some of the strengths of fatherhood is the setting of high standards, instilling discipline, forcing maturity. Children need this if they have any sort of chance to contend with the overwhelming world we live in and the reality of adulthood. But often times it goes too far and becomes overbearing and stifling. Getting that balance right is no easy task. Fatherhood impacts us all, for better or worse. There's no getting around it.

Socially, the disregard of the marginalized and outsider will lead to isolation and deterioration.

> There was a rich man who was dressed in purple and fine linen and lived in luxury every day. At his gate was laid a beggar named Lazarus, covered with sores and longing to eat what fell from the rich man's table. Even the

dogs came and licked his sores. The time came when the beggar died, and the angels carried him to paradise. The rich man also died and was buried. In Hell, where he was in torment, he looked up and saw Abraham far away, with Lazarus by his side. So, he called to him, "Father Abraham, have pity on me and send Lazarus to dip the tip of his finger in water and cool my tongue, because I am in agony in this fire."—Luke 16:19-24 (niv)

What a request. Just a little water for the privileged elite. Too up tight, arrogant, and holy to see and open up to the disenfranchised outsider.

50
Resentment and Anarchy

What precisely is the difference between freedom and chaos? "Liberalism defines government as tyrant father but demands it behave as nurturant mother."—Camille Paglia, *Sexual Personae: Art and Decadence from Nefertiti to Emily Dickinson*, (USA: Yale University Press, 1990), 3.

Fleeing from authority and rules, in hopes of being free from them once and for all can never be completely true. Chasing the wind, dreams and sensuality without a solid foundation under you is a serious problem. Pretending like it isn't will lead to disenfranchisement and death.

Even flying is regulated by strict natural laws.

The value of pursuing the infinite moves you out and away from structure. That value is good only if it is in relationship with the value of structure at the same time.

No structure means no hierarchy. With no hierarchy there is no goal, and therefore no meaning. There is just being left out and at the bottom. Resentment resides right here at this point, waiting.

Resentment towards those who are put together and positioned better, becomes a force. Viewing the structure and those better positioned, only as evil, will lead and leave you to your own hell.

Believing that the line drawn between good and evil is around your value of the infinite and freedom without the value of structure and aim will due you in. Why is it so difficult to get this right?

There are two shadow tendencies related to openness: deconstruction and being overly compassionate for the oppressed and disenfranchised.

The left's insistence on inclusivity, tolerance and essentially universalism, champions this value through identity politics, critical race theory, woke-ism, black lives matter, transgenderism, and LGBTQ ideology. They draw the moral line between them and those who draw moral lines.

So, no matter how much the left detests the hierarchy and the strict defining lines drawn by them, they have to use the hierarchy's value of drawing dividing lines to devalue them. This becomes inconsistent and self-contradictory. It ironically demonstrates that orderliness or hierarchy as such, is a permanent and eternal value.

In their book, *Attachments*, Dr. Tim Clinton and Dr. Gary Sibcy state,

> Ainsworth's studies scientifically supported this claim: A baby's cry is hardwired. It is not a sign of weakness or overdependency. And a mother cannot be too responsive to her infant. Infants of mothers who were most responsive and most sensitive during the first year of life were much more likely to become securely attached.
>
> ... Secure babies become just the opposite of what folks like Erica expect: They are more autonomous, and they cry less, explore more, and are much less clingy than their insecure counterparts.
>
> On the other hand, insecure babies were more likely to have insensitive, poorly responsive parents—parents like Erica, who is well intentioned but views her baby's cues as signs of defiance and manipulation . . . not as a way of communicating needs. These kinds of parents usually have infants who grow up to be more demanding, more whiny, more defiant and even aggressive, and less likely to be appropriately dependent in relationships.—Dr. Tim Clinton and Dr. Gary Sibcy, *Attachments: Why You Love, Feel, and Act the Way You Do*. (Nashville: Thomas Nelson, 2009), 32.

If basic consideration of something like developmental stages isn't taken into account when relating and caring for a child, significant damage can be done, no matter how good the intentions.

The experts seem to suggest a progression. In infancy there should be complete dependence. all compassion, no hesitancy and no separation. The parent should be pulling and keeping the infant close.

By year eighteen, there should be significant independence, high expectation and pushing the adult out. relating to an adult psychologically or emotionally like they are an infant and vice versa can be catastrophic.

Compassion and empathy applied at the wrong time, to the wrong person can be detrimental. It can have the opposite effect of what may be trumpeted. Virtue signaling, "standing for" the minority and oppressed has become quite the fad.

I've begun making a list of people, most of whom are professionals, who fit in the leftists' category of minority and oppressed, but who don't hold to the leftists' framework of morality.

The list includes people such as Bari Weiss, Dr. Rima Azar, Ayaan Hirsi Ali, Dave Rubin, Thomas Sowell, Coleman Hughes, Abigail Shrier, Burgess Owens, Larry Elder, Amala Ekpunibi, Katharine Birbalsingh, Brandon Tatum, and many more. They are immigrants, female, ethnic minority, or LGBTQ.

They, like many others, argue that compassion and empathy for the marginalized and oppressed, as well as identifying individuals primarily by group categorization, is actually demeaning and patronizing. It's condescending and infantilizing.

They point out things like, policies of the welfare state have fallen into the category of the overprotective mother. They state that the liberal left completely misses the significant point that empathy and help doesn't just stop working at a certain point but ends up hurting and enslaving.

These particular critics of the left, all recognize the absolute devastation of having a shallow and unsophisticated critique of systems, the wealthy, hierarchy, privilege, structure, or majorities.

If the moral framework proposed by this leftist ideology is composed of power dynamics and identity politics, then what are we to make of those listed above? They fit the criteria for being morally virtuous inside the leftist framework because they are in an oppressed identity group. But they don't hold to that framework. On the contrary they criticize it.

The leftist ideology has no place for them, and ironically casts them out.

In child development, there is a point when the child should move from dependence to independence and not be overtaken by the over protective mother or parent. The father plays a vital role in this development by relating to the child with rough house play, among other things.

The story in the Old Testament about when Jacob wrestles with God and wins; God changes his name to Israel, which means, "The one who wrestled with God and man and won."

This story and name, is a center point of how God wants us to see, understand, and relate to Him. It should not be missed or understated.

The patriarch, Israel, God's chosen people, the way of salvation, the lineage that produces the Messiah, the chosen one, is named "the one who wrestles." Wow! That's weird.

It's a brand, a title, that matches the nature of the trinity and marks out Jesus as the one who suffers, yet triumphs.

Salvation is first a legal contract. It's set, in stone. It's justification. It's a moment of conversion and regeneration. It's instantaneous. It's a status change.

Second, it is being in a dynamic relationship, constant tension, contending and fighting with sin, the world and Satan. It's being sanctified. It's a process.

Then, lastly, it is ultimate triumph, victory, celebration and being glorified.

This is the pattern of who God is, how He functions, and how He has created. It is the description that defines God Himself. It is the description of why He functions the way He does and why He designed reality like He did.

So, when there is an overcompensation of provision for a subject without leading them to contend and struggle upward and outward to growth and development, whether in the life of a child, a neighbor, or in the political society, then it ends up doing the opposite of what is seemingly intended.

This is why conservative thinkers will say that equality of opportunity is good, which allows maximum freedom for the individual, but equality of outcome is morally and functionally wrong. Because it will require force from the state or system. This will infringe and tyrannize the individual's freedom and impose a particular result.

We have seen and are seeing how this gets played out in societies. We don't have to look far. The concepts and laws of socialism and communism are fresh in our history and right in front of our eyes today.

I'm in the middle of reading through the horror stories from the book *The Gulag Archipelago* by Aleksandr Solzhenitsyn. He gives us an inside view of the work camps from the Soviet Union. I was alive when the Soviet Union collapsed.

These ideas, if not checked, lead to hell very quickly. And the scary thing is, they are coming out of a place of seemingly good intention and compassion; inside a framework made up of group identity and equality of outcome.

We have got to stop thinking about evil and evil that is acted out in terms of being in its own separated, isolated category of reality; far removed from who and what we are and what we value.

Evil is intricately tied to what we value and desire.

We aren't evil simply because we are all around bad and desire bad things. We are evil in part because we don't value and pursue all that is good for all time. There is division between all that is good, and that which values only part of the good over and above other parts to the point of ignoring, denouncing, hating, and cursing them. That is a denial of who and what God is as a triune being and you being designed in his image.

Resentment is so subtle. It is so deadly. Resentment detests being in a worse situation than others. It's wishing and working to bring them down to suffer alongside you. It most often does it without trying to be noticed or by being under the guise of goodness. Or having the appearance of being productive and beneficial.

Compassion and empathy for the disenfranchised can be used to cover the resentment.

The road to hell is in fact paved with good intentions, says the old adage.

Deconstructing with no true value of order and structure rooted in the eternal God the Father, will lead to anarchy and hell. But you will have no gratification being there, even if you know you are there with others you resent. Hell will have you in torment alone.

Postmodernism and Marxism

Before we can critique postmodernism, which many have done in the last few decades, we have to understand what it is and what it's rooted in.

We have already spent some time looking at the nature of truth. Truth is both fixed and absolute as well as open and infinite.

Postmodernism seems to be the reaction to the aspect of truth being absolute.

The motivation to push back so that there is emphasis on the infinitude aspect of truth, is a good one. The problem occurs when there is severance between both facets by trying to define truth only in one sense. That seems to be the problem with postmodernism.

Relativism is the dominant dogma of the day. All that matters is, what is true for you. There is an infinite number of ways to interpret the world. Who is to say that one way is better than another?

Postmodernism seeks to contend with the complexities of infinitude. Infinitude does pose real problems. I can barely walk down the chip aisle in the grocery store without being overwhelmed by the number of options.

The claim that one thing, out of an infinite number of things, is preferred, better or best, technically or morally, is quite a claim. But even with strong support and argument, it still seems to be quite audacious in the face of an infinite number of options.

The value and structure of rank ordering truths, beauty and goodness is all criticized by postmodernism. The critique happens of literature, history, the arts, and the sciences.

The concepts found in the work of Karl Marx, that hierarchies and rank ordering is just a power play by those who have the power, seems to have an added layer of explanation. So that when added to postmodernism's critical nature, they combine to form a very powerful and potent way of viewing reality.

Postmodernism states that there can't be any real consensus on what is true, good, and beautiful.

Marxism says that the only real thing determining what is true is force, and power groups.

The result of these two ideas joining means that the reason there is any rank ordering, hierarchy, or higher position, is because someone used power to move themselves up and push others down.

The correct or moral response to this then, is to use force to equal everything out. Tear those above down and use any means necessary to move those out and beneath, in and upward.

It doesn't matter what the group division is, as long as power is the perceived determining dividing line. It used to be a class division of the proletariat and the bourgeoisie. But it has continued to expand and morph into identity politics.

Identity politics draws lines between groups of people based on majority/minority, ethnicity, sexuality, or economics. The dividing line is a moral one that determines who is good and who is evil depending on what side of the line you are on.

The group you are in, whether majority or minority, male or female, person of color or not, able body or not, will determine if you are in the group of privilege, perpetrator, victim, oppressor or oppressed. And that is how we know who is good and who is evil.

Sounds quite primitive to me.

Using a position of authority to hurt someone by using or abusing them is wrong and evil.

Because of Postmodernism's lack of a metanarrative, it has ended up falling for the Marxist ideology; Which views every instance where there is higher and lower position, or in and out groups, as determined by power plays and as a result evil in need of rectification.

The Bible does recognize and emphasize the evil that is present when positions of authority are used to crush and victimize the weak and the vulnerable. It's a significant theme in the story line, rightly so.

But to take that theme and make it the entire framework of morality, as though the line between good and evil is drawn between the powerful and the weak, is to make a grave mistake. It is horrid hermeneutics.

Is power really the determining moral factor, the only determining moral factor, in the relation between people, structures, society, family and relationships?

That sounds like it's rooted in an idea of the cosmos coming into existence out of nothing, based on nothing and evolving by a mindless, unguided process, that becomes survival of the fittest.

Power is a factor in morality; but framing the entire moral structure by it is one of the dumbest, evil, and now looking back on the twentieth century, bloodiest ideas of all time.

Where did these ideas originate?

Postmodernism is considering the infinite. Marxism is considering the less fortunate. Both of those emphases are correct and good, rooted in the nature found in the Holy Spirit's role and function eternally.

What makes them evil is them being severed from the hierarchical, orderliness, and holiness of God the Father. The Father becomes the enemy, needs to be torn down and condemned to hell.

Equity or equality of outcome becomes the vision of heaven then.

There's just one problem.

If you get your concept of God wrong, you will get your concept of utopia and heaven wrong. If you get your concept of heaven wrong, you will most certainly find yourself in hell.

Postmodernism, coupled with Marxism, doesn't simply think that there is a downside of objective truth or hierarchy. They think that those concepts and realities themselves are evil.

What about competence? Is a hierarchy of competence allowed?

I grew up in church. The dominating description of Satan, the Devil, was that pride and arrogance was the root that birthed and caused his downfall. He thought he was better than God and decided he could be God better than God was. This resonates, no doubt.

But how about this; was Satan a postmodern Marxist?

Of course not. Satan is ancient and Marx was a modern philosopher primarily interested in political economics.

However, Marx's ideas were rooted in some sort of worldview. Certainly, in some ancient concepts.

Did the Devil create his own morality based on class division and see himself as inferior and oppressed by God, who was up the hierarchy and obviously had all power? Did he have moral grounds to resent God and want to tear Him down to produce equality?

Was that what he pitched to Eve?

Is that the framework Cain stood on to justify killing his brother?

Was that the undercurrent of Jobs' friends when they came to comfort him, but ended up using their theology to accuse him?

Is that what Solomon noticed in the mother who tragically lost her son and why he ruled against her because of her resentment? If there was inequality between her and the other mother, then pursuing equity would be the correct value and end, Right? That's what postmodernism and Marxism says.

Ideology produces a shadow. It takes a part of reality and makes it the totality. The lines drawn between right and wrong then, are wrong, because they only see the world through a partial lens.

God's moral framework and lines of right and wrong are drawn between Him as a whole and that which is separated from Him as a whole.

Blindness isn't just present by the inability to see what's bad, but by only seeing a part of all that is good.

Evil, then, isn't just produced by the love of what is bad, but by the value and pursuit of a good that is limited, narrow, severed from all that is good for all time.

God, have mercy. We have made a mess.

51
Sexuality

Introduction
Before we take a look at an always significant subject matter, let's preface it.

Sexuality is extremely personal.

Sexuality is one the most fundamental elements that define us as human. We know this innately.

The claim that our sexuality makes up a significant part of our identity, is quite true. It's understandable then why we have such strong conviction, emotion and moral claims around our sexuality.

The drive to have our sexuality normalized, no matter our sexual self-identification or how we act it out, is good and right. This is because it's a testament to the significance of sexuality as such, and the central role it plays in the human being.

Sexuality is extremely powerful.

Sex drive is constantly arguing that there is something good that needs to be pursued. The degree of that drive is supposed to be as strong as it is.

However, sex drive, similar to other human fundamental desires, reminds us that we aren't in control to the degree we thought we should be.

When's the last time you tried a three-day water-only fast, or tried to cut out sugar for several days? Go ahead and try that and watch yourself through the process. You are not in control.

We should be careful when we are quick to justify our actions and desires. When they lead us to places that we hadn't quite initially planned, we may be motivated to find a way to label them good and beneficial, because the alternative of bearing the responsibility of self-discipline, or confession and repentance would be far too difficult.

We all empathize with each other on the fact that our human desires are powerful and oftentimes control us rather than the other way around. We are all in the same boat at that fundamental level. The particulars vary, but we are all keenly aware of our failure to be in control of the varying elements and desires that are composed in the human.

What is sexuality?

Hetero, the prefix in heterosexual means, other, another, or different.

In the first chapter of Genesis, we read, "Then God said, 'Let Us (Father, Son, Holy Spirit) make man in Our image, according to Our likeness . . .' So, God created man in His own image, in the image and likeness of God He created him; male and female He created them. And God blessed them [granting them certain authority] and said to them, 'Be fruitful, multiply, and fill the earth.'"

—Genesis 1:26–28 (amp)

Homo, the prefix, and the prefix in homosexual, comes from the Greek word *homos*, meaning the same.

In the second chapter of Genesis, it states, "Now the Lord God said, 'It is not good (beneficial) for the man to be alone; I will make him a helper [one who balances him—a counterpart who is] suitable and complementary for him.' . . . For this reason, a man shall leave his father and his mother, and shall be joined to his wife; and they shall become one flesh"—Genesis 2:18, 24. (amp)

The dramatization of the man leaving the unity of the father and mother to move out and unite with the woman, is depicting the reality of the unified Godhead sending the Son into the world to be united to the human. It is also, and even more fundamentally, depicting the function of the trinity; the Father sending out the Son to unite with the Spirit who has gone out before.

Homosexuality

So, what of homosexuality?

Some would argue that sexuality, emphasized and contained inside a relationship between a man and a woman, has been understood as the highest good and the correct norm for all of history.

When that norm is regulated further by the confines of a marriage relationship, then on the surface or at first glance, the push away from that norm or tradition, into something risky, different, edgy, rebellious, could be seen as freeing, liberating, fresh, renewing or progress.

But is it?

It's the liberals who are pro homosexuality. Why?

Homosexuality in the West, for the moment, has been identified or defined as being a minority or marginalized category; being outside the norm, and therefore in need of care, protection, warmth and compassion. This is the value of the liberal.

Homosexuality is also the pushing out away from tradition, the norm of the culture and society. There is a desire for freedom, away from the confines of covenant, law, commitment and/or tradition.

It's not just the liberals who are pro homosexuality. Our growing secular society, even in Christianity, have demonstrated the value of sexual liberation. The overbearing confines of a marriage covenant have no value, demonstrated by how normal divorce is today.

Even with the value of sexual revolution, to the point of valuing and accepting homosexuality, among other forms of identity and expression, there is still a pull back to a fundamental norm. How else can it be explained that homosexuality seeks to be accepted and recognized even by the state and mimic the traditional legal and spiritual marriage relationship?

If Homosexuality is wrong, what makes it wrong?

If God condemns it, what could the reason be?

Is it arbitrary?

"It's wrong because God said it's wrong."

That as an explanation has great value and explanatory power; but needs to be demonstrated as that. God speaking is a deep theological function that is good and true, as we have noted earlier, in relation to God as the Word and one who speaks. But, what God says, still has to be coming from something reflective of His nature.

Why can't the love defined in a relationship between a husband and a wife be pursued in the relationship between a man and a man or a woman and a woman?

Love is love, after all.

God is. He is good, true, right, living, and eternal. He is the one true God, because He exists as a triune God. He is the personal-infinite God, mediated by the Son. Order as masculine, open as feminine; bound together to produce and continue to be, forever.

Homosexuality attempts to find love and union by clinging to that which is its same. Order with order, open infinite with open infinite. This doesn't work. It technically does not work.

What seems to be a value of progress and the value of liberalism, is actually and technically regress.

God has already taken into account the values of both structure and order with openness and beauty, when He creates man for woman and woman for man, and then places them in a covenant, dynamic relationship.

Any attempt to move the pieces around and reconfigure, even while labeling it advancement, progressivism or liberation, is actually destroying sexuality and the essence of relationship.

God is holistic. He has already figured how to maximize and uphold freedom and expression to its fullest for all time; and it's not by making beauty a stand-alone or freeing sexuality from all restrictions. This is a guaranteed failure.

The way for sexuality to be celebrated and expressed in all of its glory and power for the longest period of time is configured in how God has engineered male and female as a pattern after himself as an everlasting God.

The reason God designed and instituted the most intimate relationship in marriage between a man and a woman, and why He hates divorce, is because it establishes the centrality of union, imaging God as a unified being in three persons.

Divorce, adultery, fornication, sexual immorality along with homosexuality, all corrupt the goodness, purity and pleasure of sexuality and intimacy.

Male with male, order with order, structure with structure, cannot stand by itself. It's a guaranteed path to death. Female with female, open with open, infinitude with infinitude, cannot function by itself. It is a guaranteed pathway to death.

Not just death generically speaking, but death to the human as a species, technically speaking.

If we made homosexuality the priority, the normalized ideal, a good to pursue, it would threaten human existence.

Reproduction

Reproduction, as we have looked at in previous chapters, is intricately tied to the nature of God. It is all wrapped up in the intimate relationship between the sexes, which all together display the one true triune nature of God.

Homosexuality severs reproduction from the equation because reproduction comes from the union between the two different sexes, which mirrors the trinitarian nature and function of God. Severing reproduction from the equation that is supposed to display the fullness and glory of God, is the denial and betrayal of the Son, the second person of the Trinity as the eternal reproduction of God. Homosexuality then, is anti-Christ, by definition. It exchanges the truth and glory of God for a lie (see Romans 1), technically speaking.

To state it explicitly, homosexuality is in opposition to who God is as a particular triune being. Anything that isn't aligned with what God is should be judged and done away with, and God does this.

The reason is simple. If God is the source of what good is and is the source of what continual good living is, including everlasting life, then to try a means of life that isn't rooted in or patterned after what God is and how He functions will fail and do significant damage along the way.

At multiple levels of analysis, homosexuality may be narrow minded, selfish. It prioritizes the particular human, individuality, up and above humanity in a detrimental way.

Is homosexuality sexist?

Why isn't it a subtle, passive aggressive insult and disrespect to womanhood for a man to choose to pursue an intimate and sexual relationship with another man?

Could the same be said for assuming the female role and identity as a man, and vice versa, in transgenderism?

What could lead to thinking and believing that it's not just okay, but good?

Conclusion

All of us seem to want to find the defining lines of who and what we are. Once we get a handle on that, we try to be as true to that as possible. There is goodness and truth in that.

But if we are incomplete or cut off from the fundamental reality that gives us our form and value in the first place, namely God himself, then our pursuit of understanding and commitment to ourselves, whatever the aspect of life, even in our sexuality, will lead to discontentment, distortion, and deterioration.

Self-identifying is detrimental. It's the doubling down in our limited, twisted, blind, selfish identity and value that does us in. Whether it's in our sexuality, our political wing, or our theological doctrinal beliefs.

Truth is always operating between the ordered known and the open infinite. He connects us to the one who is always true, because God is personal infinite always.

Conservatives who double down, get stuck. Liberals who double down, become lost.

Being in an echo chamber isn't the value of unity and love. On the contrary, it's rooted in and the demonstration of blindness, division, and hate. It's the same thing that makes things like racism and homosexuality wrong.

Homosexuality is the dramatization of clinging to a partial aspect of reality, a denial of the others, and therefore a shadow; an evil, deadly shadow.

Sexuality is personal, no doubt. It matters. It is important. It is one of the most significant things that defines and makes up the human being. But severed from the reality that is life giving, it will be a sure dead end.

Lift that burden, and carry it to the God who is whole, complete, and able to rectify what is missing, broken, and deadly.

Real love can be found and lived in, in God, because love finds its origination in the reality that God is triune, three persons, defined in particularity, and each person valuing and relating to the other two persons eternally.

52

Love

The value of openness and freedom in isolation, doesn't value it enough. Because its existence and life span are dependent on structure and tradition, along with the mediating entity. The only way to value it in full is to value its relational counterparts. The same goes for the orderly and conservative.

Conservative fundamentalist, is it settled, absolute and a closed case? Or is it open for discussion, further investigation and more to be understood? It's both.

If you cling to absolutes and are dogmatic, you are, ironically, making the same detrimental error as the postmodern relativistic universalist, the one you are opposing at the other end of the spectrum. You have ideology, not truth. Truth is a living mediator between absolutes and the infinite, always.

Conservatives or orderly types, judge morality by attainment and separation, which is holiness.

Liberals, people who are open, judge morality by care and accommodation, which is hospitality.

God's moral framework is the value and pursuit of both.

Change and transformation doesn't mean improvement. It could mean deterioration.

Conservation and preservation don't mean holiness. It could mean stagnation.

Satan and demonic beings accuse and allure. They divide and devour. Those sit in the structure/open framework. The evil ones reside on either side in both domains, actively destroying.

If the shadows, the evil triad, emerging as a result of wrong or lack of relation to each other, are: Arrogance and Tyranny, Resentment and Anarchy, Deceit and Division, then the opposites would be:

Care, demonstrated by provision and protection. This is what the left leaning want and need from the right.

Gratitude, demonstrated by support and celebration. This is what the right leaning want and need from the left.

Truth and love demonstrated by sacrifice and unity. This is what we all want and need from everyone, first accepting the responsibility to act it out ourselves.

"For the time will come when people will not tolerate sound doctrine and accurate instruction [that challenges them with God's truth]; but wanting to have their ears tickled [with something pleasing], they will accumulate for themselves [many] teachers [one after another, chosen] to satisfy their own desires and to support the errors they hold, and will turn their ears away from the truth and will wander off into myths and man-made fictions [and will accept the unacceptable]."—2 Timothy 4:3–4 (AMP)

Ouch. Sounds like the algorithms that are hard at work on your social media accounts.

"The first one to plead his case seems right, until another comes and cross-examines him."—Proverbs 18:17 (amp)

We all fall prey to the positive feedback loop or the echo chamber. This isn't about "those other people," This is about me, us, our brand, our type.

A key ingredient, "Trust. Trust is . . . life."—Sant, Gus Van, *Good Will Hunting*, USA: Miramax, 1997, Film.

There are actual reasons for the two opposing sides not to trust one another. The division between male and female, conservative and liberal, conscientious and artist, orderly and open. If one pulls too hard in his direction, tries to dominate, and overemphasize, things can be led to hell, really.

The need for tension, relationship, back and forth, dialogue, or wrestling, requires that you emphasize your point and your side. But if you mistake your viewpoint or your side for the fullness of truth or love, then you become the problem, first and foremost.

You have failed to recognize that, in the words of Aleksandr Solzhenitsyn, "If only it were all so simple! If only there were evil people somewhere insidiously committing evil deeds, and it were necessary only to separate them from the rest of us and destroy them. But the line dividing good and evil cuts through the heart of every human being. And who is willing to destroy a piece of his own heart?"—Solzhenitsyn, Aleksandr. *The Gulag Archipelago*, New York: Harper & Row Publishers, 1974, 75.

We think people do evil because they're evil, different from me. People do evil, oftentimes, because they think they're good, doing good; and that brings us a lot closer to them than we would like to imagine.

How do you determine then, when to trust or who to trust?

The place or the person to trust is the one who is open to critique, the one who embodies confession, and has faith in the entirety of truth and love. Not a pushover, and not blind stubbornness.

Open, liberal people are convinced that love is compassion. Orderly, conservative people are convinced that love is justice. Love is both.

> If you [only] love those who love you, what credit is that to you? For even sinners love those who love them. If you do good to those who do good to you, what credit is that to you? For even sinners do the same. . . . But love [that is, unselfishly seek the best or higher good for] your enemies, and do good, and lend, expecting nothing in return;—Luke 6:32–35 (amp)

> Love endures with patience and serenity, love is kind and thoughtful, and is not jealous or envious; love does not brag and is not proud or arrogant. It is not rude; it is not self-seeking, it is not provoked [nor overly sensitive and easily angered]; it does not take into account a wrong endured. It does not rejoice at injustice but rejoices with the truth [when right and truth prevail]. Love bears all things [regardless of what comes], believes all things [looking for the best in each one], hopes all things [remaining

steadfast during difficult times], endures all things [without weakening]. Love never fails [it never fades nor ends].—1 Corinthians 13:4–7 (amp)

Why is love stated throughout history and across cultures as the most valuable reality? What is love anyway, and why is it?

And now there remain: faith [abiding trust in God and His promises], hope [confident expectation of eternal salvation], love [unselfish love for others growing out of God's love for me], these three [choicest graces]; but the greatest of these is love.—1 Corinthians 13:13 (amp)

We have spent some time defining and discussing the nature of Truth. Truth not only is that which is defined, known, objective and matter of fact, but is open ended. It's in relationship with the infinite.

Truth however sits primarily in the known and order domain. It crosses into the unknown domain just enough to not be stagnate and dead, but living and active. Truth has to work.

"Does it work?" If so, it's true. Its functionality is a testament to its validity.

Truth is both a stand-alone and in unique and vital relationship with Love.

Love sits primarily in the Open/infinite domain. Love is outward, other directed. It's optimistic. It leads with emotion and passion. It's demonstrated and acted out.

Love is a stand-alone and linked back to, overlaps and is in vital connection to truth. It grounds the open, optimistic, passion, and action towards another, to what is right, correct, technically good and actually beneficial.

"Love is discerning, desiring, and doing what is best for another, regardless of personal cost."—Charles W. Lyons

Discerning (mind, reason, God the Father)
Desiring (heart, emotion, God the Holy Spirit)
Doing (will, action, God the Son)

Beloved, let us [unselfishly] love and seek the best for one another, for love is from God; and everyone who loves [others] is born of God and knows God [through personal experience].

The one who does not love has not become acquainted with God [does not and never did know Him], for God is love. [He is the originator of love and it is an enduring attribute of His nature.] By this the love of God was displayed in us, in that God has sent His [One and] only begotten Son [the One who is truly unique, the only One of His kind] into the world so that we might live through Him.

In this is love, not that we loved God, but that He loved us and sent His Son to be the propitiation [that is, the atoning sacrifice, and the satisfying offering] for our sins [fulfilling God's requirement for justice against sin and placating His wrath].

Beloved, if God so loved us [in this incredible way], we also ought to love one another.

No one has seen God at any time. But if we love one another [with unselfish concern], God abides in us, and His love [the love that is His essence abides in us and] is completed and perfected in us.—1 John 4:7–12 (amp)

I just heard this quote the other day. I don't know who said it, "People want to go to heaven, but no one wants to die."

My boss has a line, "Everyone wants a job, but no one wants to work."

Everyone wants love and peace, but no one wants to sacrifice and suffer.

Love is what it is because it is found and intricately all wrapped up in who and what God is, existing in three persons, Father, Son, and Holy Spirit. Jesus, the Son, is the answer because he rightly contends eternally between the other two and is sent out to us as the one to connect us to God.

We are made in the image and likeness of this eternal highest defined entity. This gives us our value and meaning. We matter.

Who we are and what we do matters because we are tied to God, by nature. This is deep and meaningful. It's also devastating.

We decided to disassociate ourselves from God. Try to be human without our humanness being all wrapped up in and tied to God. That's technically impossible. It's a fatal decision.

If our being, our life, our human existence doesn't match, align with, reflect truthfully the God that we are made in the likeness of, who is perfect and good and right eternally, then we deserve to be judged. It is technically good and right to be judged for this. If good is good and right is right, then I, we stand guilty, worthy of conviction and sentencing.

Truth is all wrapped up in the nature of God.

But God is also love. And this love is demonstrated by God, in God, in history, for us, even in our right guilty conviction. This is great news.

We are separated, severed from God. God as the eternal holistic good. This foundational severance produces the disintegration, deterioration, and breakdown of all parts in the created order. We end up being broken apart and unable to live in unity, harmony, and love.

The masses are committed to view, operate, and judge, according to only an aspect of reality. They are not pursuing the difficult process of what it means to view and live-in reality with all that is good, beautiful and right, namely a God who is triune.

What precisely is the difference between freedom and anarchy?

Freedom is in an intimate relationship with order.

What precisely is the difference between order and slavery?

Order is in an intimate relationship with freedom.

Conclusion

Genesis 1:1, "In the beginning God created the heavens and the earth." (csb)

God is a singularity and multiplicity. He's not just a singularity amidst multiplicity. He is both singular and multiplicity. One being three persons. A being and infinite in being.

So, when God creates the heavens and the earth, He is not only creating multiplicity from singularity, which includes many things that mirror Him. But even deeper than that, He builds singularity and multiplicity into the creation. Even more than that, He doesn't just do it one way or at one level, but in innumerable ways and with several layers which all somehow exist harmoniously.

"God created the heavens"—the infinite, transcendent, uncontainable, multiplicity.

"And the earth"—the finite, local, bounded, singularity.

God isn't just adding when creating. He is implementing multiplication or the mechanism of reproduction, which more fully represents and reflects him as one who is strictly defined, infinite, the mediation between, as well as their eternal reproduction in the Son.

The creation is a dramatization of the contention and interplay between the finite and the infinite.

Death and rebirth, regeneration and reproduction are a key central element to what God has created.

If freedom means the absolute absence of bounds and definition, then freedom itself collapses in on itself because it has a particular definition. For freedom to be real, it has to be tied to and in relationship with parameter, boundary, definition, and regulation.

If absolutism is the defining and containment of all, then ironically, it can't be trusted. For absolutes to be real, they have to contend with the absolute of the unknown, undefined, and infinite. These by definition are not known, defined, or contained.

Christianity is the true explanation then because it has as its central claim one who is absolutely defined and infinite in nature. This is Francis Schaeffer's description of God, being personal infinite.

In Genesis 1:27 it states, "So God created man in his own image; he created him in the image of God" (csb)

Pause. What is the image?

"He created them male and female." (csb)

The framework of the Father as order, the Spirit as open, and the Son as the mediating and reproduced entity, is the fundamental, eternal framework.

To review, here are a few examples; the pattern that defines sexuality as male and female is the same pattern that defines the brain's two hemispheres.

It's the same pattern that defines personality differences, which can be summed up in orderly and open types.

It's the same pattern for human inner being as mind, emotion and will.

It's the same pattern in political divisions, Eastern and Western religions, the Bible's structure of Old and New Testaments and the Gospels.

It's the same pattern in the Bible's central message of the gospel as justification, sanctification, and glorification.

This pattern matches the defining nature of the three persons of the Trinity.

Each of those is quite a significant domain of our reality. That they all have the same pattern can't be arbitrary or insignificant.

This paradox of order and chaos requires a mediating force that is of strongest operating substance and is of highest value, necessarily. The Bible holds that the central figure in reality is one who is servant/king, sufferer/overcomer, crucified and resurrection.

"Enter through the narrow gate. For wide is the gate and broad and easy to travel is the path that leads the way to destruction and eternal loss, and there are many who enter through it. But small is the gate and narrow and difficult to travel is the path that leads the way to [everlasting] life, and there are few who find it."

—Matthew 7:13–14 (amp)

The reason we are severed from all that is good, beautiful and right is because we are severed from the particular originating source that exists holistically and eternally, that produces all that is good, beautiful and right.

Bow down and worship this God, He is the one true God.

If you are lost, reach out and trust this God, He is able and willing to help and to save.

This would be right, meaningful, and true to do conceptually, philosophically, scientifically, psychologically, emotionally, willfully, collectively, personally, spiritually, and religiously.

My friends were right, I was stuck.

The lack of operation of my will, the emphasis on my thought, my fear of the unknown kept me introverted and conservative, safe and defensive.

I was still just that little kid in an unknown city, in an unknown building, hesitantly moving away from my family and walking through a mysterious doorway.

But, over the years, even in my weakness and fear, there's been a voice, a familiar voice... coming from a church building. The building, an old masonic temple. Once home to the dark and hopeless, had become filled with living witnesses to a message, a way toward the personal-infinite living God.

The voice wasn't speaking, it was singing and joined by others. It sang out, "Though you walk through the waters, I will be there, and through the flame. You'll not, no way, be drowned. You'll not, no way, be burned. For I am with you. Fear not." It was the sound of home.

Those once gathered voices have since faded. Things have grown darker. The great deep threatens. But those words, spoken by the prophet Isaiah, still ring true. Originating in God, they have found their home in the Living Word, Jesus, where there is salvation.

In the midst of the chaos and confusion, darkness and loss, not just in my life, but in our society and in this dark age, those words beckon, calling me, calling you, calling us, forward.

These words can be trusted. They come from the one who is eternally good and living, true and truth, always loving, the God of the Bible, Father, Son, and Holy Spirit.

So, that's my story, and I'm open to your interpretation.